Year 5.

USING MATHS VOCABULARY

Dictionary

for 7–11 year olds

Steve Mills • Hilary Koll

A B C D E F G H I J K L M N O P Q R S T U V W X Y Z

A B C D E F G H I J K L M N O P Q R S T U V W X Y Z

Heinemann Educational Publishers
Halley Court, Jordan Hill, Oxford, OX2 8EJ
a division of Reed Educational and Professional Publishing Ltd

Heinemann is a registered trademark of Reed Educational and Professional Publishing Ltd

Oxford Melbourne Auckland
Johannesburg Blantyre Gaborone
Ibadan Portsmouth (NH) Chicago

First published 1999

04 03 02
10 9 8

Heinemann Educational (paperback edition) ISBN 0 435 02474 4

Heinemann Library (cased edition) ISBN 0 431 06889 5
British Library Cataloguing in Publication Data 510.3

Designed and illustrated by Moondisks Ltd.
Photographs reproduced by permission of The Ancient Art & Architecture Collection (p.56) and Robert Harding Picture Library (p.57)
Printed and bound in Spain

abacus

An abacus is a counting machine.
The number of beads on each rod of this abacus tells us how many Hundreds, Tens and Units a number has.
This abacus shows 3 hundreds, 1 ten and 9 units, giving 319.

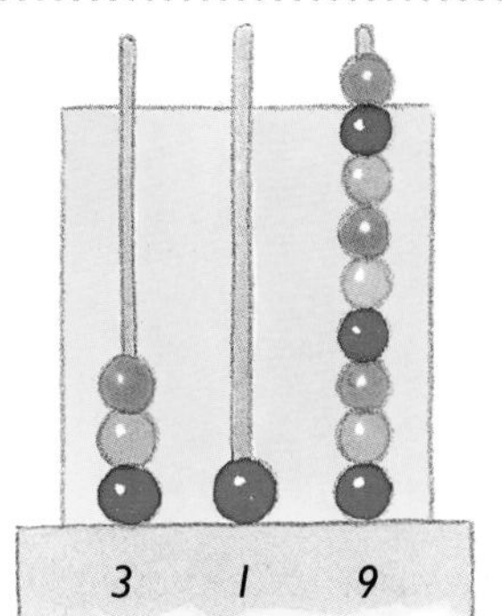

accuracy

Related word: accurate

The accuracy of a number or measurement is how exact it is.

acute angle

See also: angle, obtuse angle, turn

An acute angle is a **turn** that is less than 90° (90 degrees).

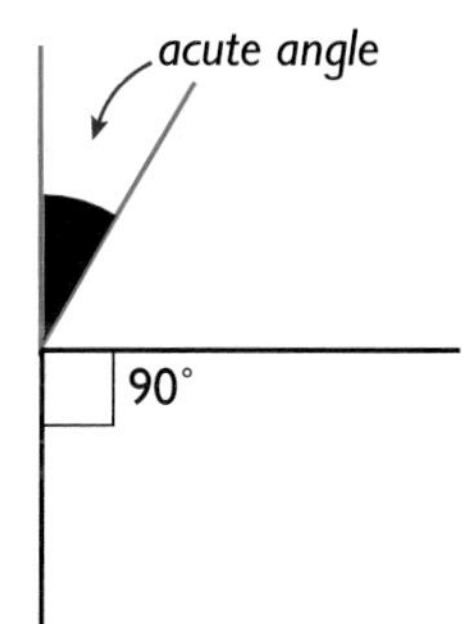

addition

See also: plus, subtraction, total
Related words: add, sum

Addition is finding the **total** of two or more numbers.
We use the **plus** sign (+) when we add numbers together.

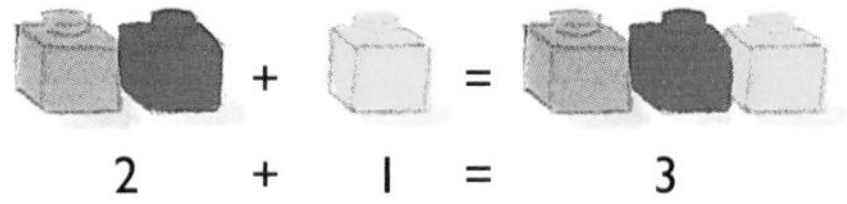

2 + 1 = 3

adjacent

Adjacent means 'next to'.

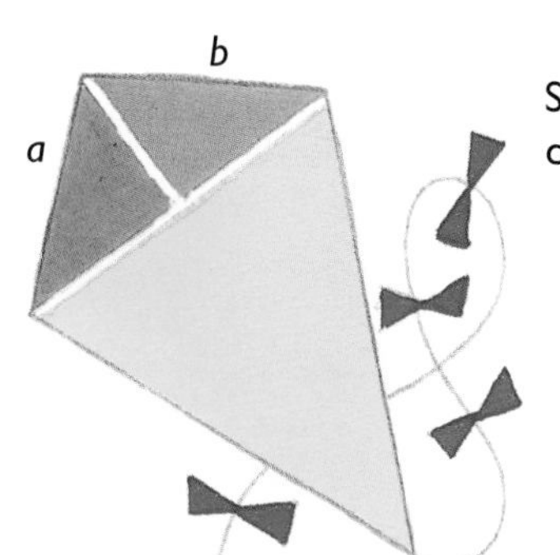

B C D E F G H I J K L M N O P Q R S T U V W X Y Z

algebra

Algebra is a part of maths where letters stand for numbers. Mathematicians use algebra to solve problems and investigate number patterns.

$$6 + a = 7$$

a is equal to 1

$$x \times 3 = 15$$

x is equal to 5

algorithm

An algorithm is the series of steps we follow to do a calculation.

alternate

Alternate means 'every other one'. One set of alternate numbers in the sequence 8, 10, 12, 14, 16, 18 can be divided exactly by 4.

a.m.

See also: p.m., twenty-four-hour clock

The abbreviation a.m. stands for *ante meridiem.* It is used to show the time between midnight and midday (noon) when we use the twelve-hour clock.

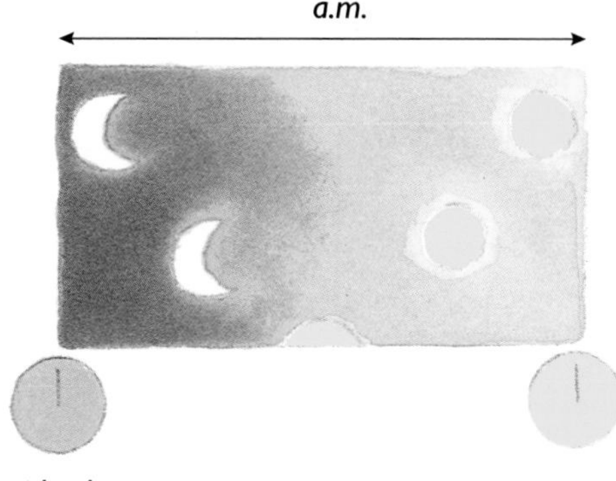

angle

See also: acute angle, degree, obtuse angle, reflex angle, right-angle, rotation, straight angle, turn

An angle is an amount of **turn** measured in **degrees** (°).

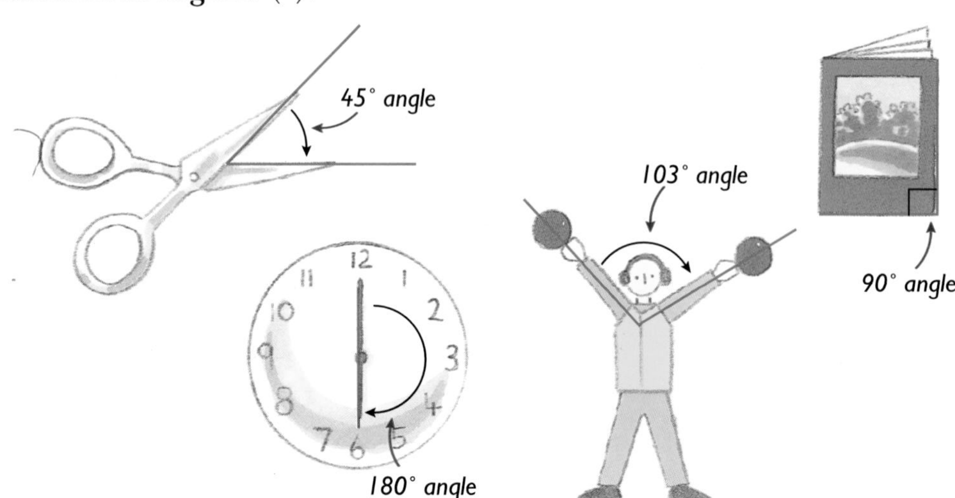

angle measurer

Related word: protractor

An angle measurer is used to draw and measure angles.

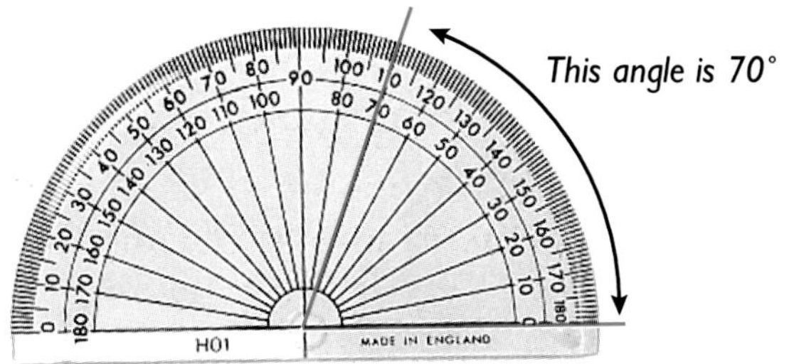

This is one type of angle measurer.

anticlockwise

See also: clockwise

Anticlockwise is the opposite direction to the way in which the hands of a clock move.

apex

The apex of a shape is the highest point.

approximation

See also: estimation

An approximation is a rough answer we get by changing parts of a calculation to make it easier to do. For the calculation 52 × 19, we might do 50 × 20 to get an approximation.

arc

An arc is a curved line which, if continued, would make a complete circle.

area

See also:
surface area

Area is the amount of surface that a shape covers. In a two-dimensional shape it is the space inside the lines or within the boundary. In a three-dimensional shape it is the total amount of surface of all the faces. We measure area in square units like square centimetres (cm^2) and square metres (m^2).

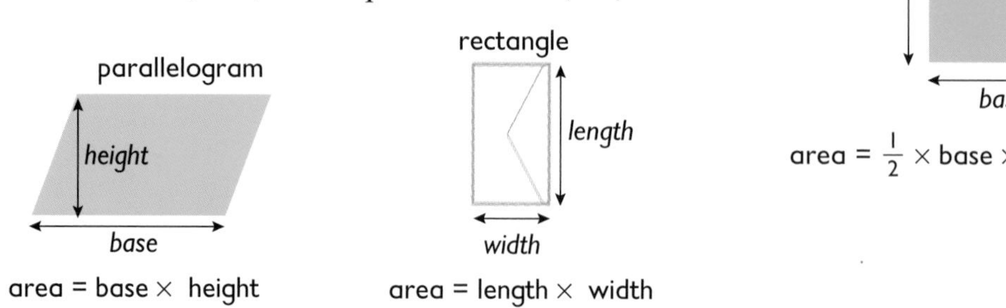

surface area of case = total amount of surface of each face
= 2 (*length* × *width*)
+ 2 (*height* × *width*)
+ 2 (*length* × *height*)

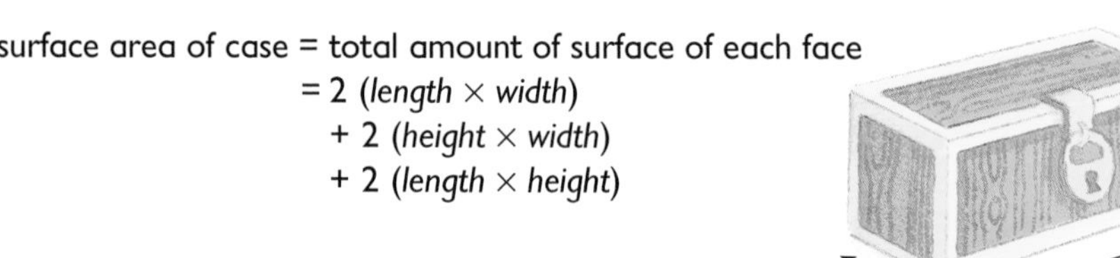

ascending order

See also:
decreasing,
descending order,
increasing

Ascending order means going upwards or getting bigger. The numbers 3, 1, 14, 6, 7 can be put into ascending order like this: 1, 3, 6, 7, 14.

average

Related word:
modal

An average is a number we use to represent a typical or middle value in a set of numbers. There are three important types of average in mathematics: **mean**, **mode** and **median**.

Alison's test scores are: 6, 6, 7, 8 and 18.

To find the mean, we add the scores together and then divide the answer by the number of scores, that is, 45 ÷ 5. So, the mean is 9.

The mode is the most popular or most frequent value. So, the mode for Alison's scores is 6.

The median is the middle value when the numbers are put in order. The median for Alison's test scores is 7. If there is no middle value because there is an even number of values, as in 2, 3, 5 and 8, the median is halfway between the two middle values, and so is 4.

axis

See also: horizontal, line of symmetry, symmetry, vertical

An axis is a straight line. The plural of axis is axes. Axis has two meanings in mathematics.

a) Graphs have two axes, the **horizontal** or *x* axis, and the **vertical** or *y* axis.

Remember which is which by saying, '*x* is a cross' or '*y* is high'.

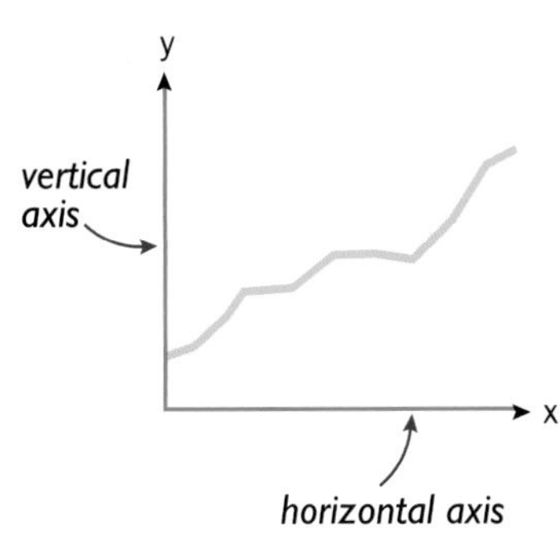

b) An axis of symmetry is sometimes called a **line of symmetry** and it divides a two-dimensional shape into two reflected halves. An axis of rotation is a line which a three-dimensional shape is rotated around.

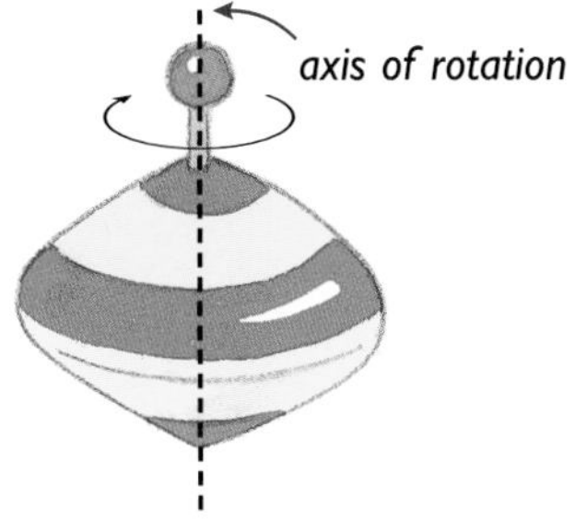

bar chart, bar graph

See also: graph

A bar chart (also called a bar graph) uses bars or columns to show information. When the bars are vertical they are sometimes called column graphs.

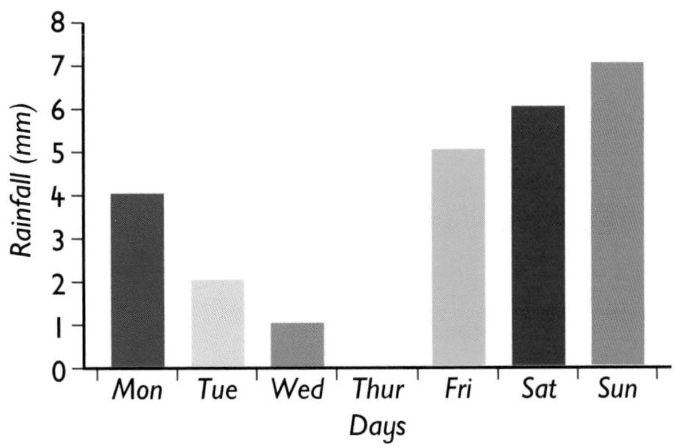

Bar graph showing rainfall in 1 week.

bar-line graph

See also: bar chart

A bar-line graph is similar to a **bar chart** but uses lines instead of bars to show amounts.

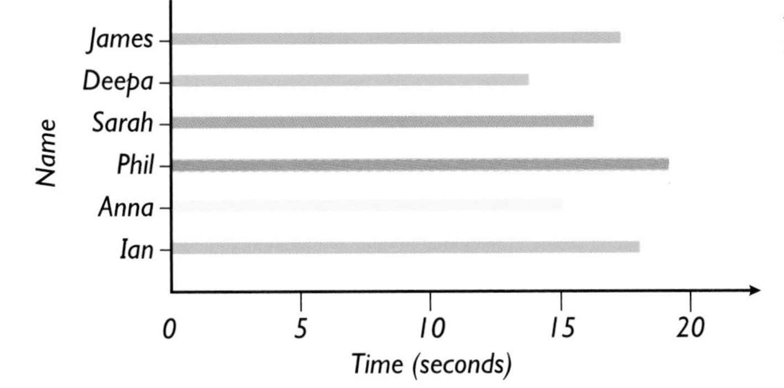

A bar-line graph showing the times of running 100 metres.

base

See also: decimal, place value

Base has two meanings in maths.

a) Our counting system uses ten as its base (or grouping number). This means we count units from 0 to 9 and then we write 10 to show one ten and no units. We write 32 to show 3 tens and 2 units. Base ten is also called the decimal system. Sometimes we use other base numbers, for example, computers use base two.

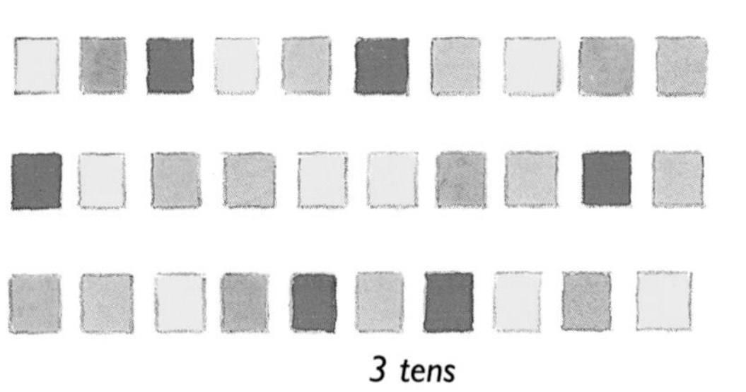

3 tens and 2 units gives 32

b) The base is the bottom of a shape. In a three-dimensional shape the base is the face on which it is resting and in a two-dimensional shape it is the line at the bottom.

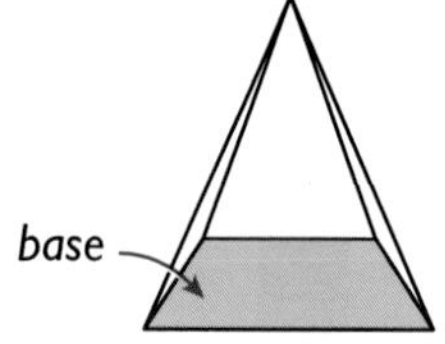

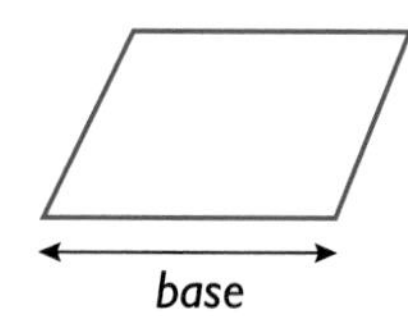

bearing

See also: angle, clockwise, degree

The bearing of an object is the **angle** it has turned from north in a **clockwise** direction. We measure bearings in **degrees** (°). When someone says, 'I've lost my bearings' it means they do not know what direction they are going in.

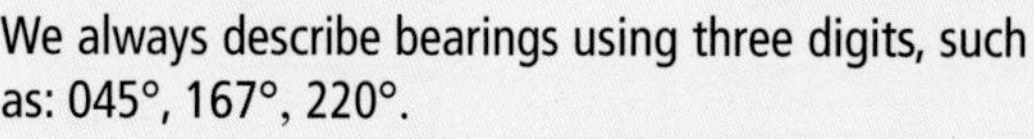

We always describe bearings using three digits, such as: 045°, 167°, 220°.

The bearing of the boat from the lighthouse is 215°.

bias

See also: equally likely outcome, fair, random
Related word: biased

Something has bias if it is unfair. A biased dice is weighted or shaped to make one number come up more often than the other numbers.

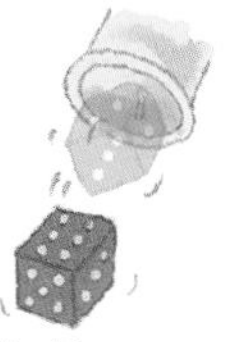

This dice might be biased because a 6 is thrown each time.

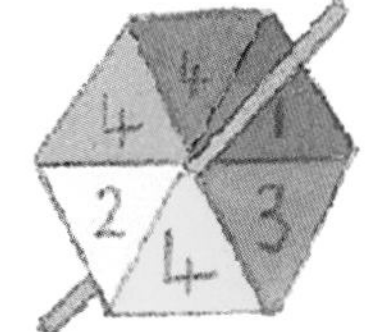

This spinner is biased towards 4.

bisect

When we bisect something we cut it into two equal parts.

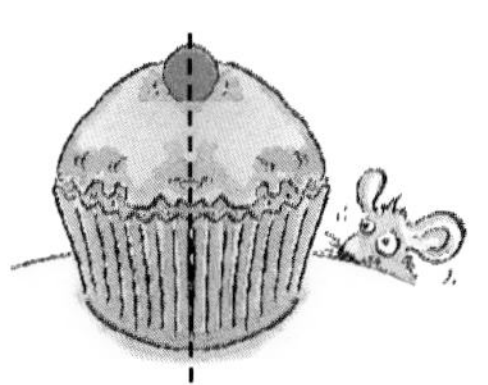

The line bisects the cake.

block graph

See also: bar graph

A block graph is similar to a **bar chart** but uses individual blocks which are joined to make columns.

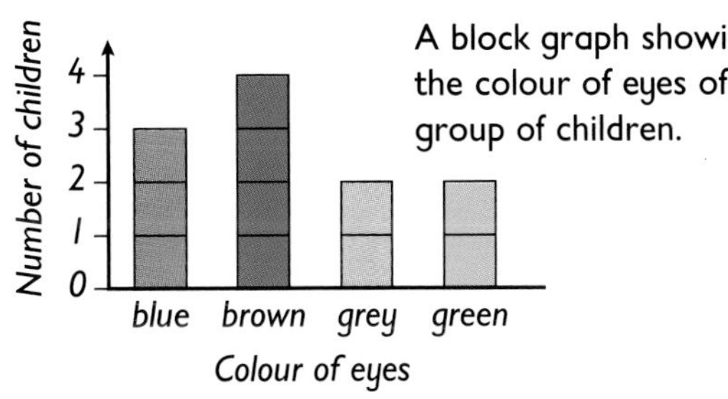

A block graph showing the colour of eyes of a group of children.

brackets

See also: coordinates, symbol

Brackets are mathematical **symbols** that look like this: ( ). **Coordinates**, such as (3, 2) are grouped inside brackets. Some number questions include brackets which often show things that need to be worked out first. For example, whether you put brackets around 4 + 3 in the following calculation affects the answer:

$6 \times 4 + 3$	$6 \times (4 + 3)$
$= 24 + 3$	$= 6 \times 7$
$= 27$	$= 42$

breadth

See also: width

Breadth is the same as **width**. It is the distance across an object measured from side to side.

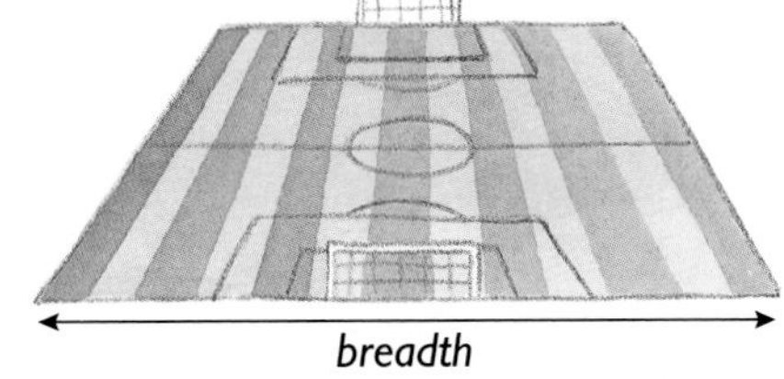

calculation

Related word: calculate

Calculation is the process of working something out in maths.

A B C D E F G H I J K L M N O P Q R S T U V W X Y Z

cancel

See also: equivalent fraction

Cancel has two meanings in maths.

a) We cancel when we divide the numerator (top) and denominator (bottom) of a fraction by the same number. This gives **equivalent fractions** with smaller numbers.

b) Pressing the 'cancel' button on a calculator will clear the display.

$$\frac{4}{20} \rightarrow \frac{4 \div 4}{20 \div 4} \rightarrow \frac{1}{5}$$

$$\frac{6}{16} \rightarrow \frac{6 \div 2}{16 \div 2} \rightarrow \frac{3}{8}$$

In the first example, we cancel by 4 (to get from $\frac{4}{20}$ to $\frac{1}{5}$), and in the secon we cancel by 2 (to get from $\frac{6}{16}$ to $\frac{3}{8}$).

capacity

See also: volume

The capacity of something is the greatest amount it can hold. We talk about the capacity of a bucket, a fish tank and a car boot. Capacity is usually measured in metric units of millilitres (ml) and litres (l) but sometimes imperial units like pints and gallons are used. Units of **volume**, such as cubic centimetres (cm^3) and cubic metres (m^3), are also used to measure capacity.

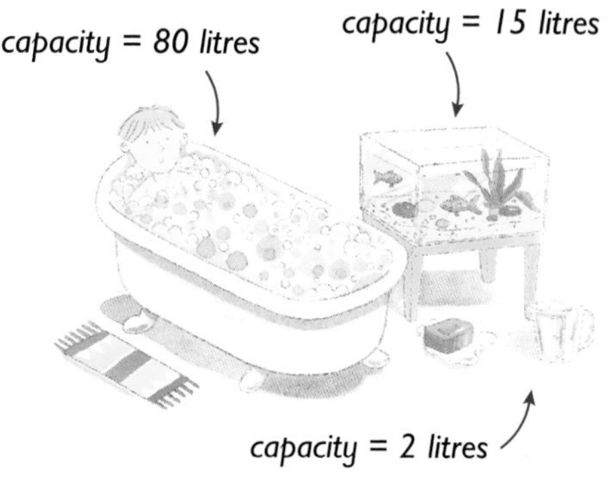

Carroll diagram

See also: Venn diagram

A Carroll diagram is a way of sorting and representing information using rows and columns. To allow everything to be sorted, one column is called, for example, 'orange' and the other column is called 'not orange'. If one row is called 'triangles', then the other row is called 'not triangles'. The Carroll diagram is named after Lewis Carroll, who also wrote *Alice's Adventures in Wonderland.*

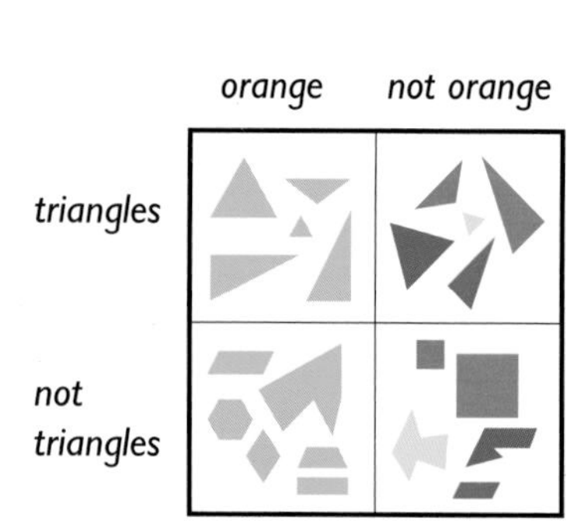

Celsius

See also: degree, Fahrenheit, scale

Celsius is a **scale** used to measure temperature. Celsius uses units of **degrees** (symbol °) and is often abbreviated to C. The Celsius scale measures 0°C when water freezes and 100°C when it boils.

centimetre

See also: distance, length, metric

A centimetre (cm) is a **metric** unit used for measuring **length** and **distance**. It is equal to ten millimetres (mm). One hundred centimetres is equal to one metre (m). One centimetre is a bit less than half an inch.

centre of rotation

See also: rotation, rotational symmetry, symmetry

The centre of rotation is the point around which we do a **rotation**.

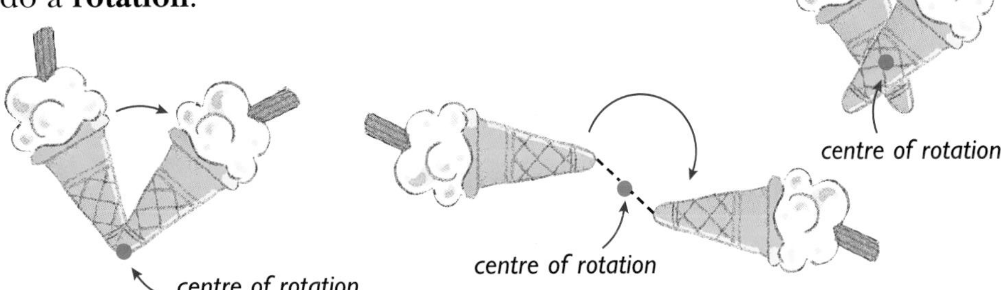

When we use tracing paper to rotate a shape or picture, the centre of rotation is the place where we put our pencil point. We then turn the paper around this point.

century

A century is one hundred of something, like a period of time that is one hundred years long or a cricketer's score of one hundred.

Cent' comes from the Latin word *centum* meaning one hundred, and can mean either one hundred of something (as in century) or one hundredth of something (as in centimetre).

certain

See also: impossible, probability
Related word: certainty

We use the word certain in **probability** to describe events that will definitely happen. July is certain to come after June. If a coin is tossed it is certain to land with either heads or tails face up.

A B C D E F G H I J K L M N O P Q R S T U V W X Y Z

chord

See also: circle, circumference, ellipse

A chord is a line which joins two points on the **circumference** of a **circle** or an **ellipse**.

circle

See also: circumference, diameter, radius
Related word: circular

A circle is a round, flat two-dimensional shape where all points on the **circumference** are the same distance from the centre.

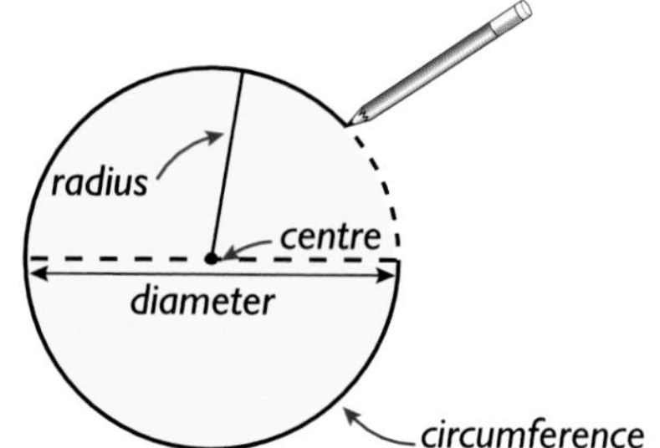

circumference

See also: circle, diameter, perimeter, pi

The circumference is the distance around a circle. It is the **perimeter** of a circle and is approximately 3·14 times longer than the **diameter**.

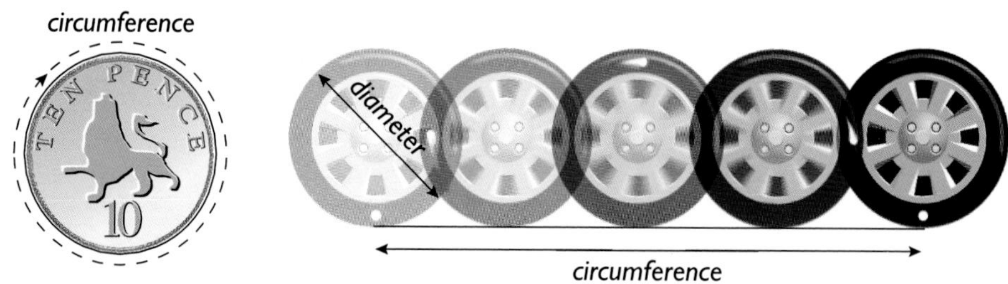

class interval

See also: data, grouped data

A class interval is the size of the groups we might use when dividing up some **data** to put in a graph or a table. To show the ages of everyone in your town we could group the data using a class interval of ten. So everyone from 0 to 9 would be grouped together, and everyone aged from 10 to 19 would be grouped together, and so on.

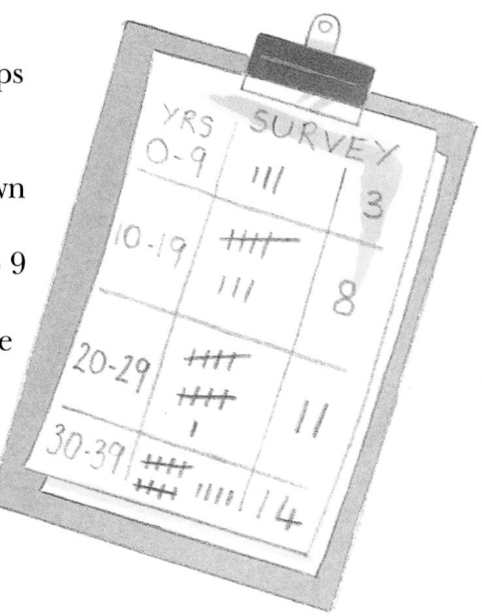

clockwise

See also: anticlockwise, turn

Clockwise is a direction of **turn**. The hands of a clock move in a clockwise direction.

column

A column is used to help us organize numbers or writing on a page. We arrange things on top of each other (vertically). Column headings are the labels for columns, and they tell us quickly what sorts of things are in the columns.

column graph

See also: bar chart

A column graph is a type of **bar chart** which uses columns to show amounts of things.

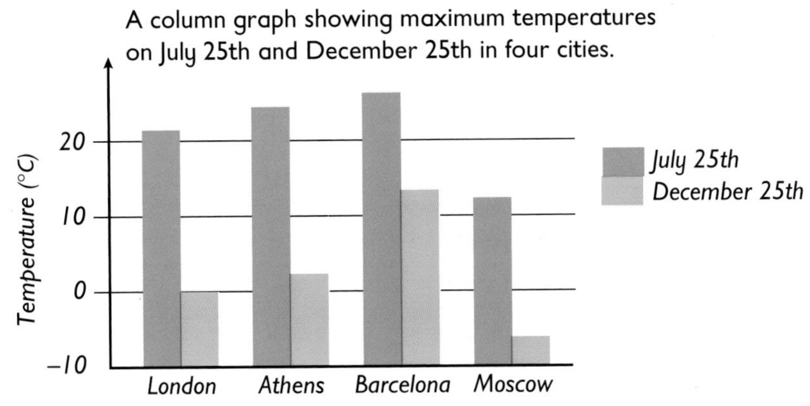

common denominator

See also: denominator, fraction

Two **fractions** have a common denominator when they have the same **denominator** (the number on the bottom of the fraction), like $\frac{1}{5}$ and $\frac{4}{5}$.

common fraction

See proper fraction.

A B C D E F G H I J K L M N O P Q R S T U V W X Y Z

compass

See also: bearing

A compass is used for finding direction. It has a magnetic needle which always points north. We can use this to find other directions. The four main points of the compass are north, south, east and west. There are other points in between these, like north-west and south-east.

compasses

A pair of compasses is used for drawing circles and arcs of circles.

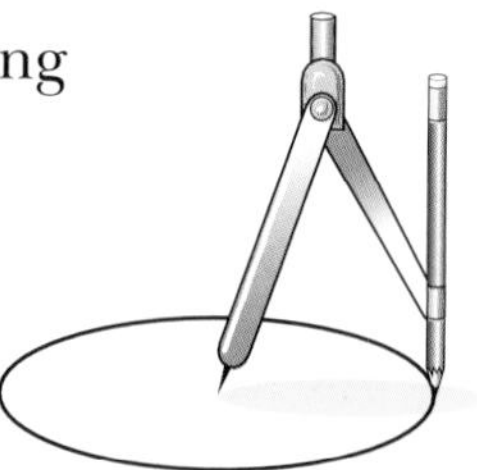

A side-on view of a pair of compasses.

concave

See also: convex, vertex

Concave means curved inwards, like a saucer or a cave. A concave two-dimensional shape has one **vertex** which points inwards.

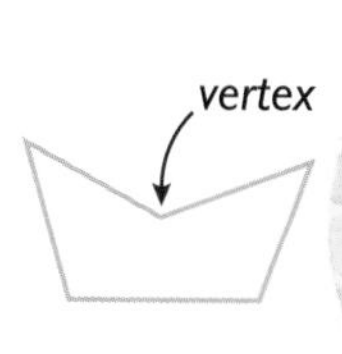

A satellite dish is concave.

concentric circles

Concentric circles all have the same centre but are different sizes, like ripples made by throwing a stone into still water.

cone

See also: base, vertex
Related word: conical

A cone is a three-dimensional shape with a circle as its **base** and a pointed **vertex**.

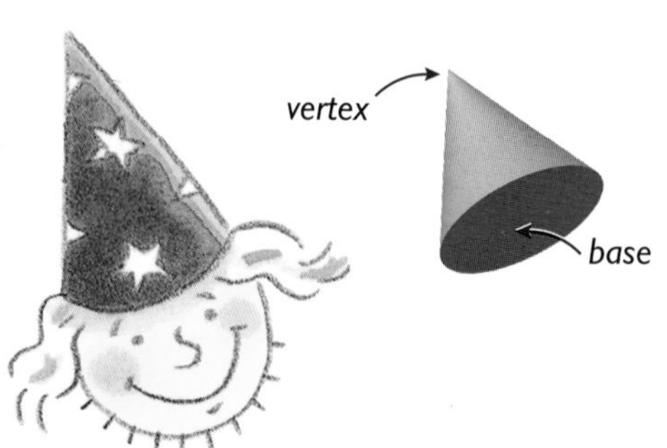

congruent

See also: similar
Related word: congruence

Shapes are congruent if they are identical to each other in shape and size, but they can be positioned in different directions.

These rockets are congruent.

consecutive

Consecutive things come one after another. May, June and July are consecutive months and 3, 4, 5 are consecutive whole numbers.

continuous data

See also: discrete data

Continuous data is information collected by measuring things, like weight, height, length, volume, temperature and age. It is called continuous data because, if we used smaller units of measurement (or a stronger magnifying glass), we could continue to measure more accurately. It is different from **discrete data** which we get by counting things, like the number of pets belonging to your classmates.

conversion graph

A conversion graph allows us to change one unit of something to another. We can use conversion graphs to change fractions to percentages, degrees Celsius to degrees Fahrenheit and Pounds to Francs. From the temperature conversion graph we can convert 0°C to 32°F and 100°C to 212°F.

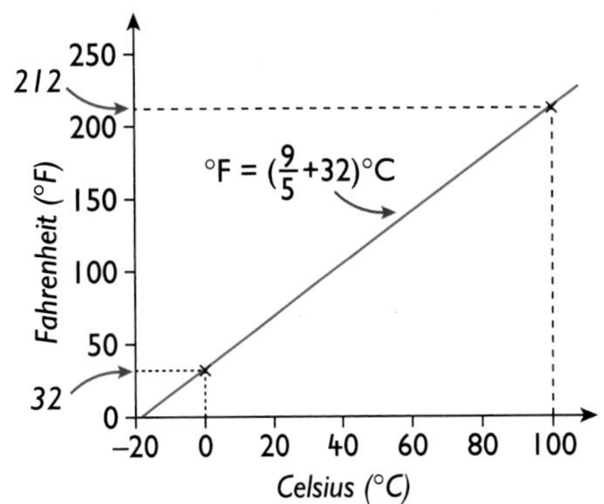

convert

See also: conversion graph
Related word: conversion

Convert means to change. If you go to another country you might convert your Pounds into a different currency, perhaps French Francs or Spanish Pesetas. In the same way we can convert fractions to decimals or percentages, so $\frac{1}{5}$ becomes 0·2 or 20%.

A B C D E F G H I J K L M N O P Q R S T U V W X Y Z

convex

See also: concave, vertex

Convex means curved outwards, like an eyeball or a hill. A convex two-dimensional shape has all its vertices pointing outwards.

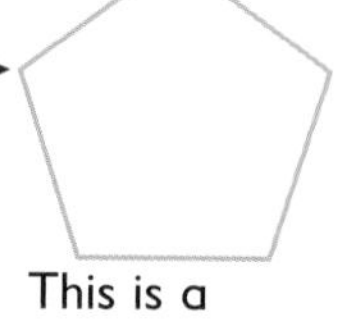

This is a convex shape.

The top of this mouse is convex.

coordinates

See also: axis

Coordinates allow us to pinpoint exactly where something is on a map or graph. They are written like this: (7, 5) or (34, 23). The first number is the *x* coordinate and shows how far along the *x* or horizontal **axis** the object is. The second number, or *y* coordinate, shows how far it is up the vertical axis.

Remember the order by saying, 'In the house, up the stairs'.

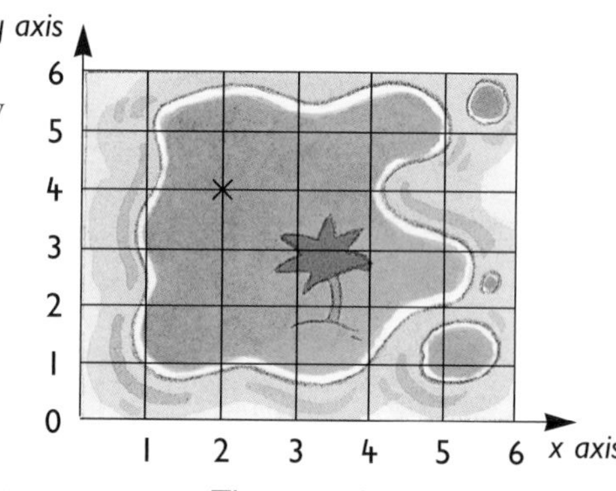

The cross has the coordinates (2, 4).

cross-section

A cross-section is a shape made by cutting straight through something, like an apple or a tree. A cross-section of a triangular prism can be a triangle or a rectangle.

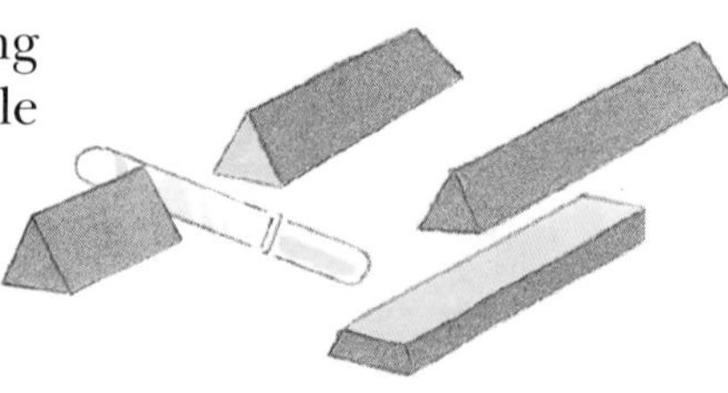

cube

See also: cuboid, rectangular prism

Cube has two different meanings in maths.

a) A cube is a three-dimensional shape which has six square faces all the same size. It is a special sort of **cuboid** or **rectangular prism**.

b) To cube a number means to multiply it by itself twice, for example $2 \times 2 \times 2$. This is also shown as 2^3 and is called 'two cubed' or 'two to the power of three'.

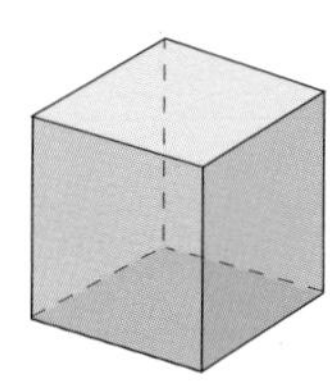

cube root

See also: square root

The cube root of any chosen number is the number that, when multiplied by itself twice, gives the chosen number. For example, the cube root of 64 is 4, because 4 multiplied by itself twice ($4 \times 4 \times 4$) gives 64. If a number is cube-rooted it looks like this: $\sqrt[3]{64}$.

cubic centimetre

See also: capacity, metric, volume

A cubic centimetre (cm^3) is a **metric** unit we use to measure **volume** and **capacity**. One cubic centimetre will hold one millilitre (ml) of liquid.

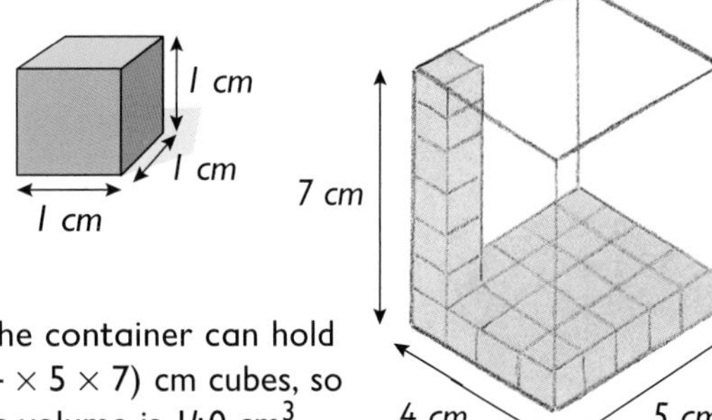

The container can hold (4 × 5 × 7) cm cubes, so its volume is 140 cm^3.

cubic metre

See also: capacity, metric, volume

A cubic metre (m^3) is a **metric** unit we use to measure **volume** and **capacity.**

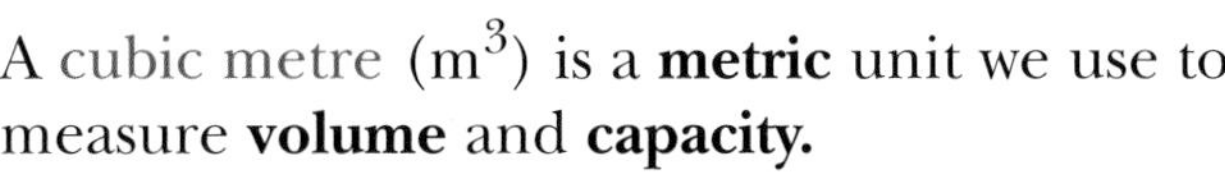

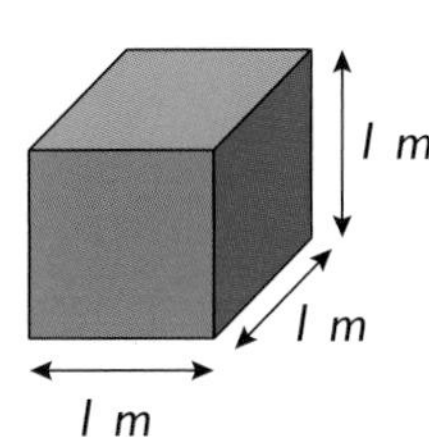

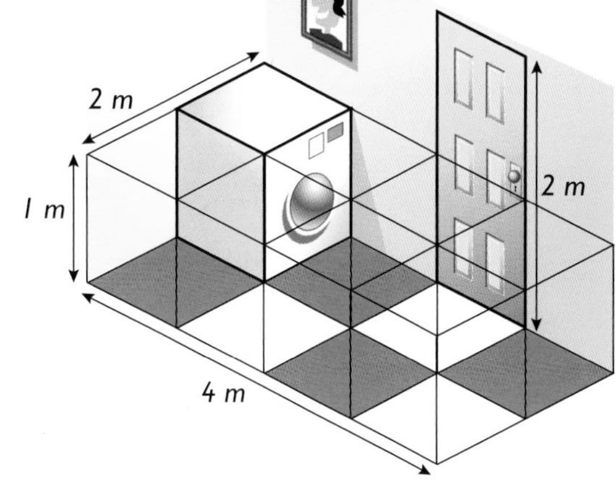

cubic number

See also: square number

Cubic numbers are numbers made by multiplying one number by itself and then by itself again, for example, 8 is a cubic number ($2 \times 2 \times 2 = 2^3 = 8$). Other cubic numbers include 1 ($= 1^3$), 27 ($= 3^3$), 64 ($= 4^3$), 125 ($= 5^3$).

cubit

A cubit is an old unit for measuring length. It is the distance from the elbow to the tip of the middle finger.

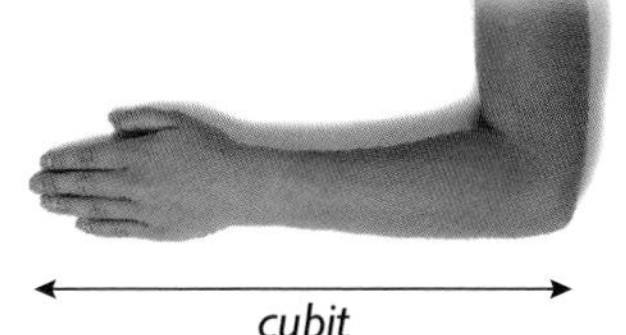

cuboid

See also: cube, rectangular prism

A cuboid is a three-dimensional shape which has six rectangular faces, like a cereal box. It is also called a **rectangular prism**.

This cow is made entirely of cuboids.

cylinder

Related word: cylindrical

A cylinder is a 3-D shape with circular ends of equal size. Cylinders include tins of fruit, rolls of toilet paper and even some coins.

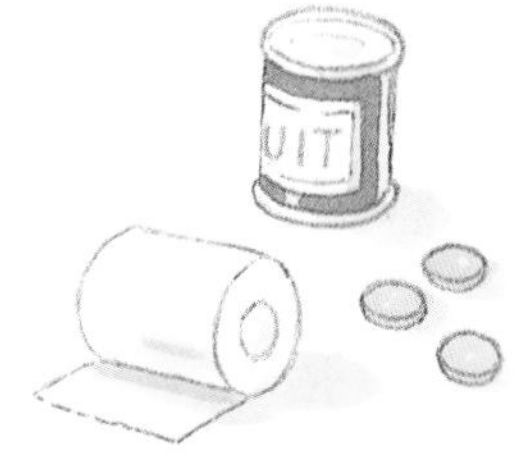

data

See also: continuous data, discrete data

Data is information about something. It can be in words – the list of names of people in your class; in numbers – football tables; or in pictures – drawings of people's pets.

decade

A decade is a period of time that is ten years long.

decagon

A decagon is a two-dimensional shape with ten straight sides and ten angles.

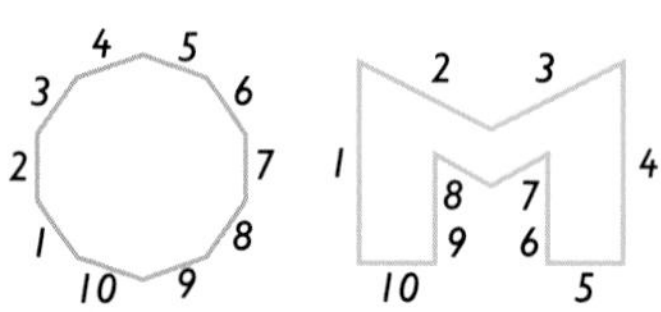

These shapes are decagons.

decahedron

A decahedron is a three-dimensional shape with ten faces.

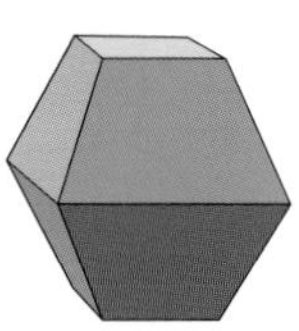

decimal

See also: denominator

Decimals are numbers like 0·2 and 3·38. They are 'part numbers' because they include amounts that are less than one. They are another way of writing fractions which have **denominators** of 10, 100 and 1000, like $\frac{1}{10}$ and $\frac{17}{100}$.

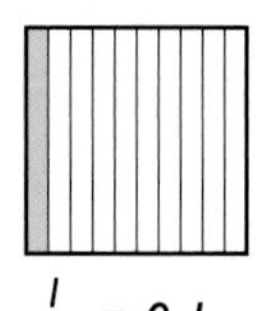

$\frac{1}{10} = 0{\cdot}1$

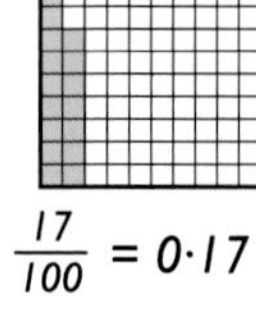

$\frac{17}{100} = 0{\cdot}17$

0·17

decimal numbers: 0·1 0·2 0·3 0·4 0·5 0·6 0·7 0·8 0·9 1·1 1·2 1·3 1·4 1·5 1·6 1·7 1·8 1·9

whole numbers: 0 1 2

decimal place

The number of decimal places is the number of digits to the right of the decimal point. The number 6·34 has two decimal places and 3·9702 has four.

decimal point

The decimal point separates whole numbers from 'part numbers' that are less than 1, for example **3·42**.

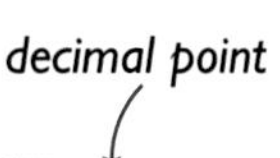

Decade, decagon, decahedron and decimal come from the Greek word for ten, *deca*.

decreasing

See also: ascending order, descending order, increasing

Decreasing means getting smaller. These cities are arranged in order of decreasing size: London, Leeds, Lincoln.

degree

See also: angle, Celsius, Fahrenheit, turn

A degree is a unit of measurement. The symbol ° means degrees. We measure **angles** in degrees; there are 360° in a full **turn**. We measure temperature in degrees on the **Celsius** or **Fahrenheit** scales.

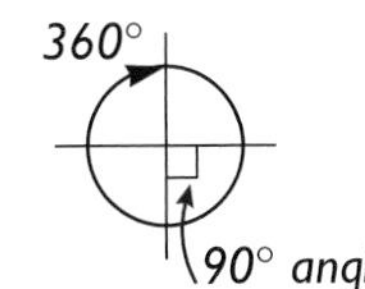

denominator

See also: common denominator, fraction, numerator

The denominator is the bottom number in a **fraction**. It shows how many equal parts the whole has been divided into. Five is the denominator in the fraction $\frac{1}{5}$.

depth

See also: length, height, width
Related word: deep

The depth of something, like a bucket or swimming pool, is a measurement of how far it is from the top to the bottom. We also use the word depth to explain the position of a fish or a deep-sea diver. He might swim to a depth of twenty metres.

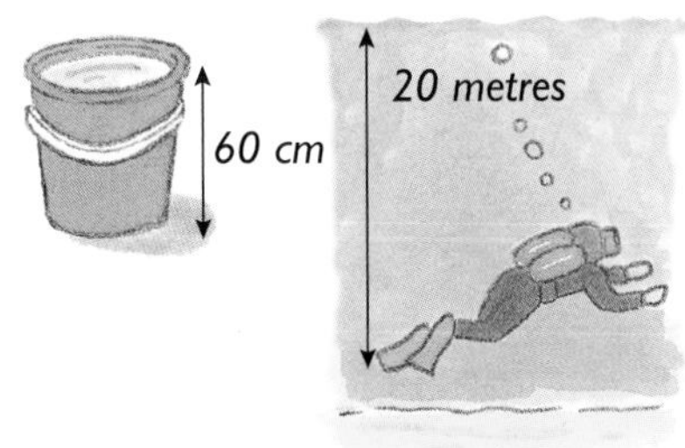

descending order

See also: ascending order, decreasing, increasing

Descending order means getting smaller. The numbers 14, 7, 6, 3, 1 are in descending order.

diagonal

Related word: diagonally

Diagonal has two meanings in maths.

a) A diagonal is a straight line drawn from one corner of a two-dimensional shape to another (but not one next to it).

b) A diagonal line is not horizontal or vertical but slanting.

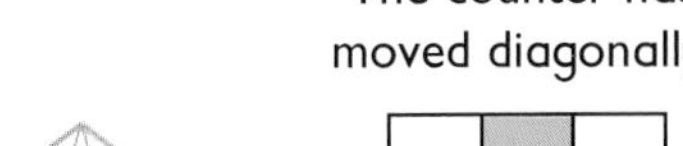

The counter has moved diagonally.

These diagonals form a five-pointed star.

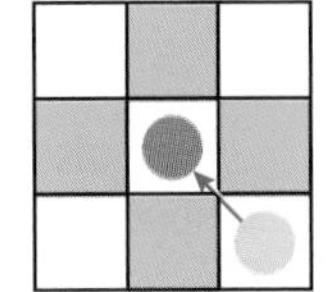

diameter

See also: circle, pi, radius

Diameter is the distance across a **circle** through the centre. It is twice the length of the **radius**.

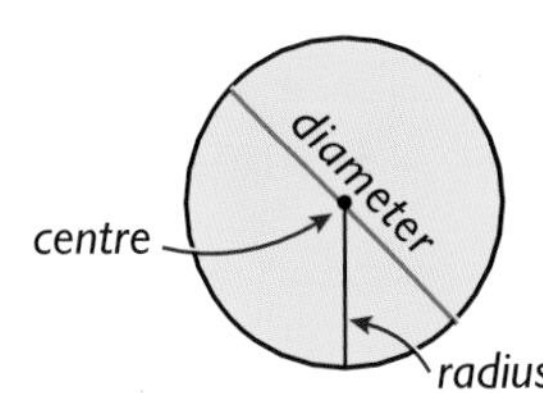

A B C **D** E F G H I J K L M N O P Q R S T U V W X Y Z

difference

See also: subtraction

The difference between two numbers is how much larger the bigger one is than the smaller one.

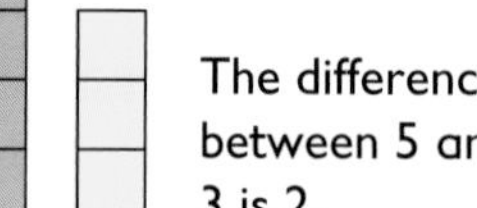

The difference between 5 and 3 is 2.

digit

See also: numeral, place value
Related word: figure

Digits are ten symbols we use to write numbers: 0, 1, 2, 3, 4, 5, 6, 7, 8, 9. In the number 358 the digits are 3, 5 and 8. How much a digit is worth depends on its place in a number. In 358, the 3 is worth 300 but in 236 it is worth 30.

dimension

See also: plane, solid shape, three-dimensional, two-dimensional
Related word: dimensional

A dimension is a measurement of size and shape. A line has one dimension – length. **Plane** (or flat) shapes that we can only draw on paper, like squares, triangles and pentagons, have two dimensions – length and width. We call these **two-dimensional**, or 2-D, shapes. Cubes, cylinders and spheres have a third dimension – height or depth, and so these are known as **three-dimensional**, or 3-D, shapes. These can be either **solid** or hollow.

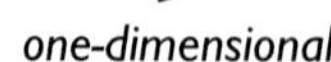

one-dimensional

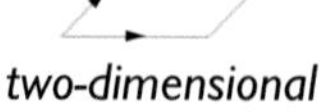

two-dimensional

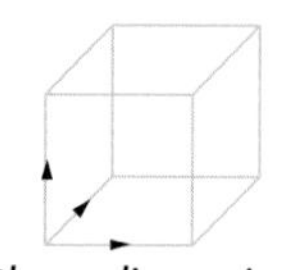

three-dimensional

discount

A discount is the amount of money taken off the full price of something. It is often expressed as a percentage of the full price.

discrete data

See also: continuous data, data

Discrete data is information we get from counting things, like the number of cars in a car park, the days in a week or the coins in our pocket. Discrete data is usually in whole numbers. It is different from **continuous data** which we get by measuring things.

distance

See also: length

Distance is a measure of how far apart two points are.

The distance from ant A to ant B is 5 centimetres.

division

See also: multiplication
Related word: divide

Division is what happens when we share things equally or divide things into equal groups. We use these symbols to show division: ÷ and $\overline{)\quad}$.

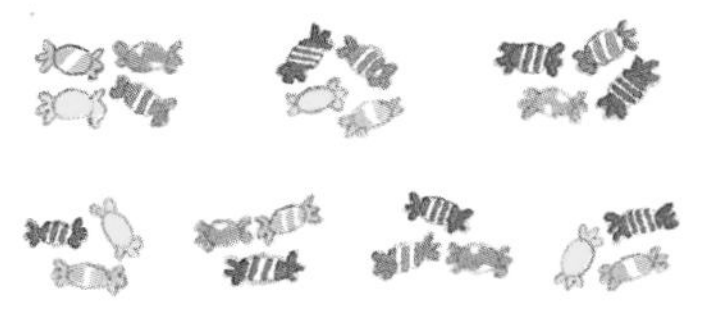

Twelve sweets can be divided into three groups of 4 sweets, or four groups of 3 sweets.

divisor

The divisor is the number we are dividing by. In both of these problems the divisor is three: 24 ÷ 3 and $3\,\overline{)36}$.

dodecagon

A dodecagon is a two-dimensional shape with twelve straight sides and twelve angles.

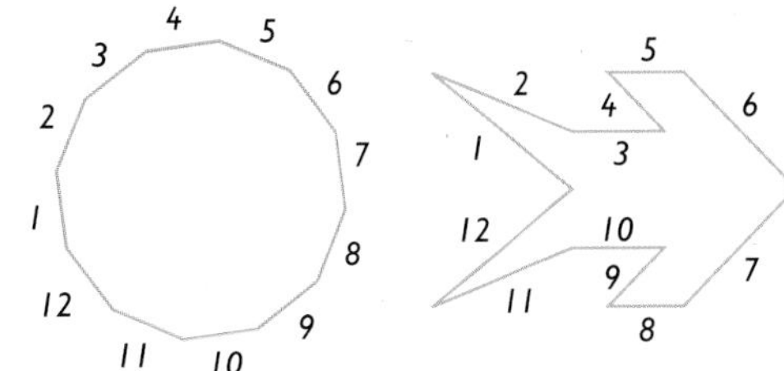

dodecahedron

See also: face

A dodecahedron is a three-dimensional shape with twelve **faces**.

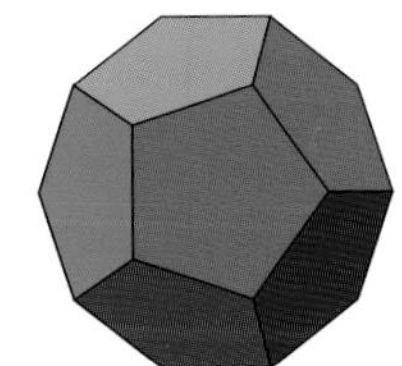

Dodeca is a Greek word which means twelve. *Hedron* is a Greek word meaning base, so a dodecahedron has twelve bases or faces.

edge

See also: face

An edge is where two **faces** of a three-dimensional shape meet. A cube has twelve edges and a sphere has none.

ellipse

See also: line of symmetry, oval
Related word: elliptical

An ellipse is a two-dimensional, **oval** shape with two **lines of symmetry**.

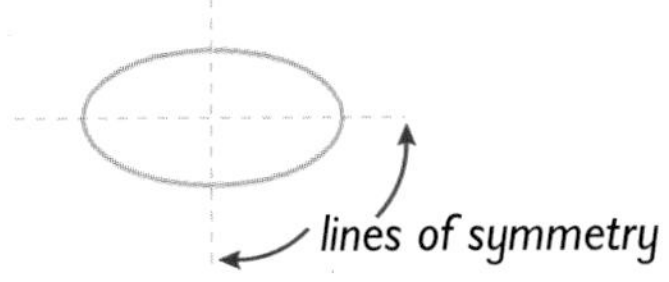

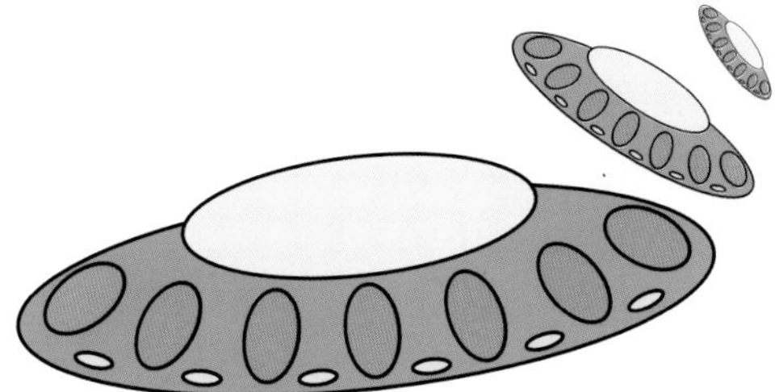

Can you see the ellipses in this pattern?

A B C D E F G H I J K L M N O P Q R S T U V W X Y Z

enlargement

See also: scale, transformation

An enlargement is a type of **transformation** that increases or decreases the size of an object without changing its shape. The picture on the right is an enlargement of the picture on the left.

equally likely outcomes

See also: bias, fair, probability, random

Events have equally likely outcomes if the chance of them happening is the same. There are two equally likely outcomes when we toss a coin (heads or tails), and six when we roll a dice (we could throw 1, 2, 3, 4, 5 or 6).

equals

Related words: equal, equality

Equals means 'the same as', so things on each side of the equals sign (=) should show the same amount, like $2 + 3 = 5$ and $8 - 3 = 4 + 1$.

equation

An equation is a mathematical sentence that uses an equals sign (=). Both sides of the sign show the same amount. These are both equations:

$3 \times 4 = 12$

$x = 6 + y$ (where $y = 1$ and $x = 7$).

equilateral triangle

See also: triangle

An equilateral triangle is a two-dimensional shape which has three sides equal in length and three angles of 60°.

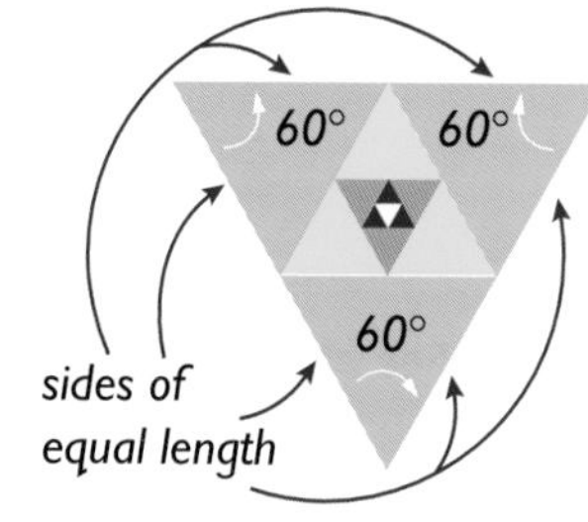

All the triangles in this pattern are equilateral triangles.

equivalent

Related word: equivalence

Equivalent means 'having the same value as', so 100p is equivalent to £1 and $\frac{1}{5}$ is equivalent to 0·2 or 20%.

equivalent fraction

Equivalent fractions have the same value even though they have different numerators (top parts) and denominators (bottom parts). These fractions are equivalent: $\frac{1}{2}$, $\frac{2}{4}$, $\frac{3}{6}$, $\frac{4}{8}$.

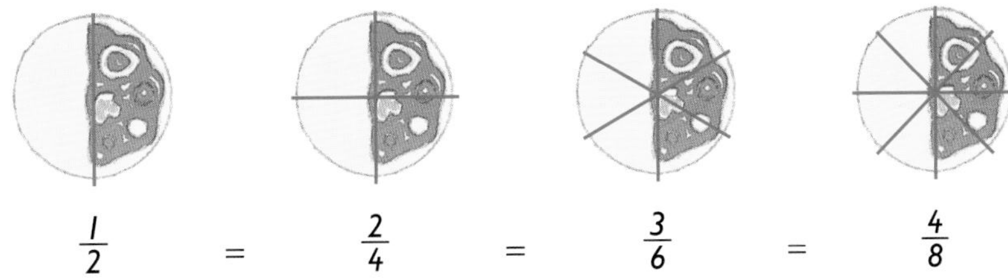

$\frac{1}{2} = \frac{2}{4} = \frac{3}{6} = \frac{4}{8}$

estimation

See also: approximation
Related word: estimate

An estimation is a good guess. We could estimate that it might take about an hour to walk three miles or that the height of a door is about two metres.

even number

See also: odd number

Even numbers are numbers that can be divided by two to give whole numbers. All numbers that end in 0, 2, 4, 6 and 8 are even.

face

A face is one of the flat or curved surfaces of a three-dimensional shape. A cube has six faces, a cylinder has three faces and a sphere has one face.

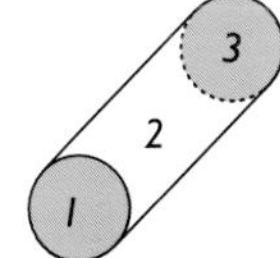

A cylinder has 3 faces.

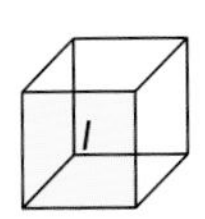

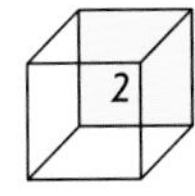

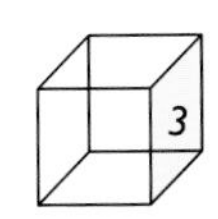

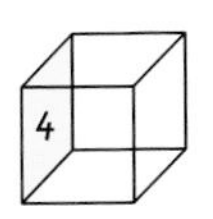

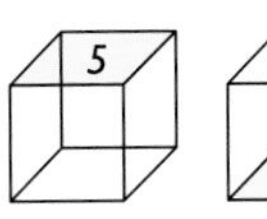

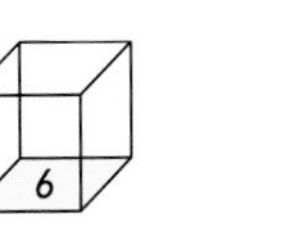

A cube has 6 faces.

A sphere has 1 face.

factor

Factors are whole numbers that divide exactly into another number. The factors of 36 are 1, 2, 3, 4, 6, 9, 12, 18 and 36.

Fahrenheit

See also: Celsius, degree, scale

Fahrenheit is a **scale** used to measure temperature. Fahrenheit uses units of **degrees** and is often abbreviated to F. The Fahrenheit scale measures 32°F when water freezes and 212°F when it boils.

Water boils at 212°F.

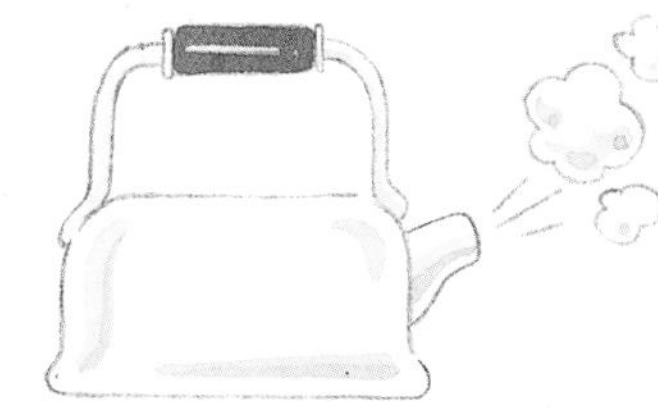

A B C D E **F** G H I J K L M N O P Q R S T U V W X Y Z

fair

See also: bias, equally likely outcomes, probability, random

We say something is fair when the outcomes are **equally likely**, that is, when no outcome is favoured in some way. A dice is fair if there are equal chances of throwing 1, 2, 3, 4, 5 or 6.

Fibonacci numbers

See also: sequence

Fibonacci was an Italian mathematician who found a special number **sequence**. The Fibonacci number sequence begins 1, 1, 2, 3, 5, 8, 13 … Each number in the sequence is formed by adding together the two numbers before it.

fifth

A fifth is one part of something that has been divided into five equal parts and is written as a fraction ($\frac{1}{5}$), a decimal (0·2) or a percentage (20%).

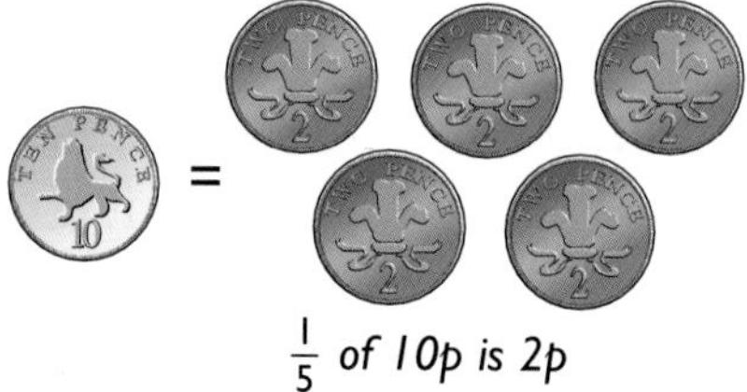

$\frac{1}{5}$ *of 10p is 2p*

figure

See digit

formula

Related words: formulae, formulas

A formula is a quick way of writing a mathematical rule.

Here are some useful formulas:
area of a rectangle = length × width
volume of a cuboid = length × width × height

fraction

See also: improper fraction, mixed number, proper fraction

A fraction is a part of something split into equal parts. Fractions are made up of two parts, called the numerator (top number) and denominator (bottom number) and are written like this: $\frac{1}{10}$.

A fraction of our class plays for the school football team.

frequency

The frequency of an event is the number of times it happens over a certain amount of time.
The frequency of your going to school is usually five times a week or the frequency of your postman calling might be six times a week.

frequency table

See also:
tally, tally chart

A frequency table is a way of recording the number of times something happens or how many of certain things we have. We might make a frequency table of vehicles passing the school or of people's pocket money. We can use **tallying** to do this.

a frequency table

geometry

Geometry is the part of mathematics that is about shapes and their movements.

gram

See also:
mass, metric

A gram (g) is a **metric** unit used for measuring **mass**. One thousand grams is equal to one kilogram (kg). Twenty-eight grams is approximately one ounce.

graph

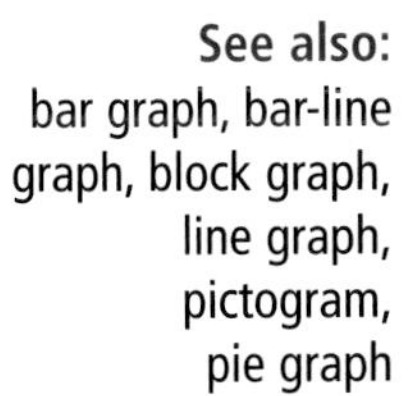

See also:
bar graph, bar-line graph, block graph, line graph, pictogram, pie graph

A graph is a way of showing information as a picture to make it more easily understood. There are many different types of graph, including **bar-line graphs**, **block graphs**, **pictograms** and **pie graphs**.

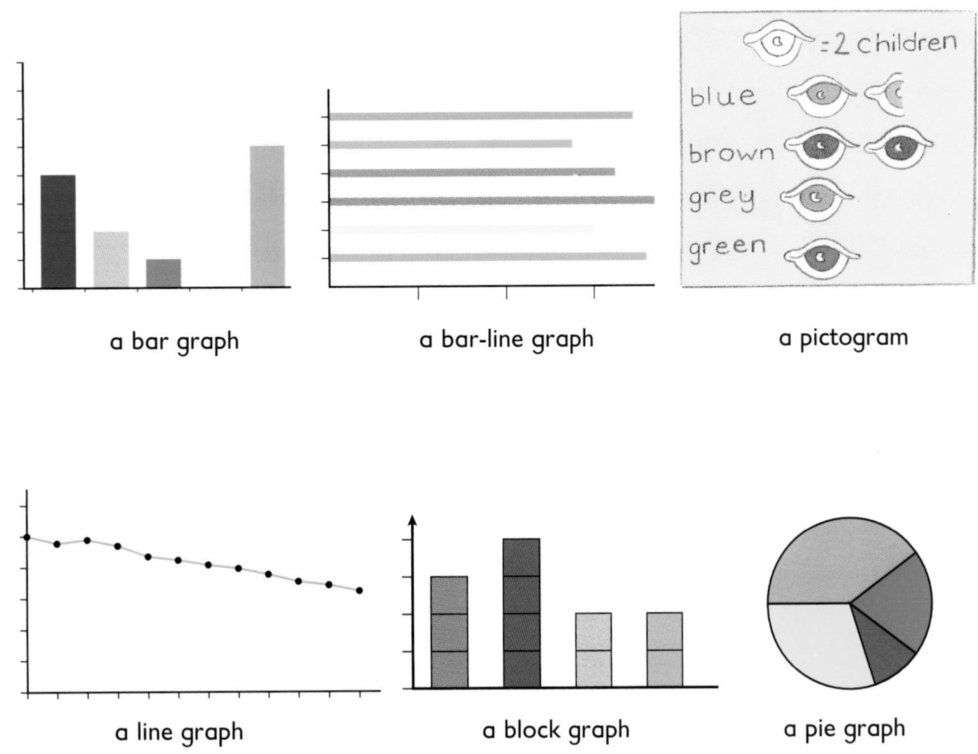

a bar graph

a bar-line graph

a pictogram

a line graph

a block graph

a pie graph

grouped data

See also: class interval, data

Grouped data is data which has been grouped together to make the information easier to understand. For example, if we want a graph to show the ages of everyone in your town we would group some of the ages together, so everyone aged 0 to 9 might be grouped together, and those aged 10 to 19 might be grouped together, and so on.

half

A half is one part of something which has been divided into two equal parts and is written as a fraction ($\frac{1}{2}$), a decimal (0·5) or a percentage (50%).

half turn

See also: right-angle, rotation, turn

A half turn is half of a full **rotation** and measures 180° (180 degrees) or two **right-angles**.

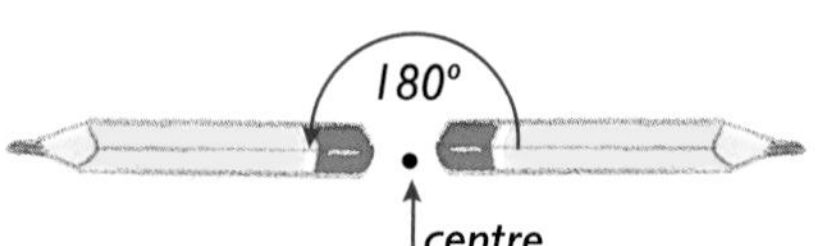

This pencil has been rotated half a turn around the centre.

height

Related word: high

a) Height is a measure of the vertical length of something, like a tree or a person standing.

b) The height of a two-dimensional shape is the distance from the top to the base.

height

hemisphere

See also: sphere
Related word: hemispherical

A hemisphere is a three-dimensional shape that is half a **sphere**. The Earth is divided into the Northern Hemisphere and the Southern Hemisphere.

Northern Hemisphere

Southern Hemisphere

heptagon

Related word: heptagonal

A heptagon is a two-dimensional shape with seven straight sides and seven angles.

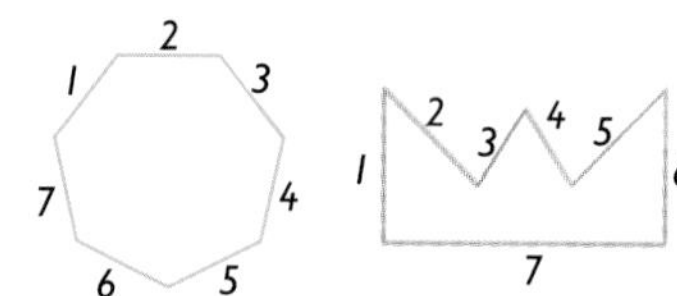

hexagon

Related word: hexagonal

A hexagon is a two-dimensional shape with six straight sides and six angles. In a regular hexagon all the sides are the same length and the angles are the same.

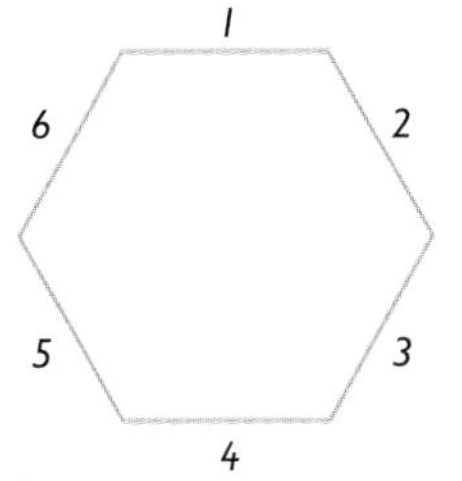

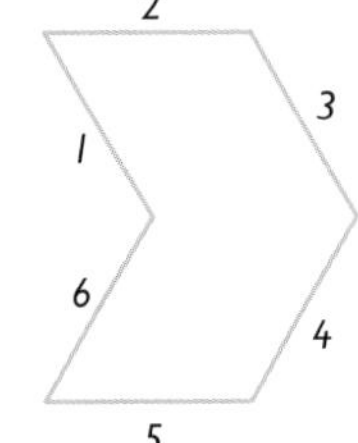

horizontal

See also: vertical

Horizontal means level or flat.

To remember which way is horizontal, think of the horizon – the imaginary line where the sky meets the land or the sea in the distance.

horizontal

hundredth

A hundredth is one part of something that has been divided into one hundred equal parts and is written as a fraction ($\frac{1}{100}$), a decimal (0·01) or as a percentage (1%). In decimal numbers, they are written in the column to the right of the tenths column.

Th	H	T	U	t	h
		2	5		
2	7	8	4		
		1	4	2	3

icosahedron

An icosahedron is a solid, three-dimensional shape with twenty faces.

Icosahedron comes from the Greek words *eikosi* meaning twenty and *hedra* meaning base.

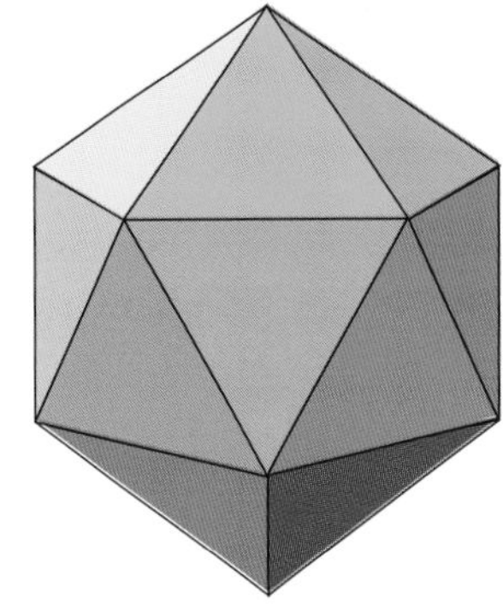

imperial, imperial units

See also: metric

Imperial units are part of an old measuring system that is different from the **metric** system. Here are some imperial units:

length	12 inches (in) = 1 foot (ft), 3 ft = 1 yard (yd), 1760 yards = 1 mile
capacity	8 pints (pt) = 1 gallon (gall)
mass	16 ounces (oz) = 1 pound (lb), 14 lb = 1 stone (st)

Comparing some imperial and metric units
12 inches is about 30 centimetres (cm)
1 yard is a bit less than 1 metre (m)
1 mile is approximately 1.6 kilometres (km)
1.75 pints is approximately 1 litre (l)
1 pound is about 0.45 kilogram (kg)

impossible

See also: certain, probability

We use the word impossible in **probability** to describe events that will definitely not happen. It is impossible for the day after Monday to be Friday, or for pigs to grow wings and fly.

improper fraction

See also: fraction, proper fraction

An improper fraction has a numerator (top number) that is larger than the denominator (bottom number), like $\frac{3}{2}$ and $\frac{7}{4}$. These fractions are also called top-heavy fractions and are more than one whole.

$\frac{1}{2} + \frac{1}{2} + \frac{1}{2}$

$= \frac{3}{2}$ *(three halves)*

increasing

See also: ascending order, decreasing, descending order

Increasing means getting larger. These numbers are arranged in increasing order: 2, 4, 9, 21, 22, 103.

Ranjit's height is increasing.

infinite

If something goes on for ever we say it is infinite. Numbers are infinite because we can always add one to (or subtract one from) whatever number we have. We use the symbol ∞ to show infinity (and –∞ to show negative infinity).

integer

See also: negative number, whole number

An integer is a **whole number** and can be either more or less than zero or equal to zero. These numbers are integers: –8, –3, 0, 12, 36.

intersection

See also: Venn diagram
Related word: intersect

Intersections are places where things cross or overlap. The point where two lines cross is the intersection. On **Venn diagrams** an intersection is where two circles overlap.

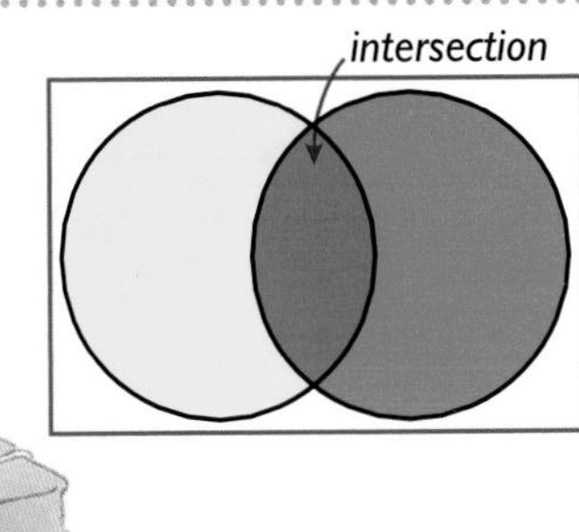

intersection

inverse operation

The inverse is the opposite. The inverse operation to addition is subtraction and vice versa, because each 'undoes' the other. Multiplication and division are also inverse operations.

irregular

See also: regular polygon, regular polyhedron
Related word: irregularity

A two-dimensional shape is irregular when its sides or angles are not equal. A three-dimensional shape is irregular if its faces are different.

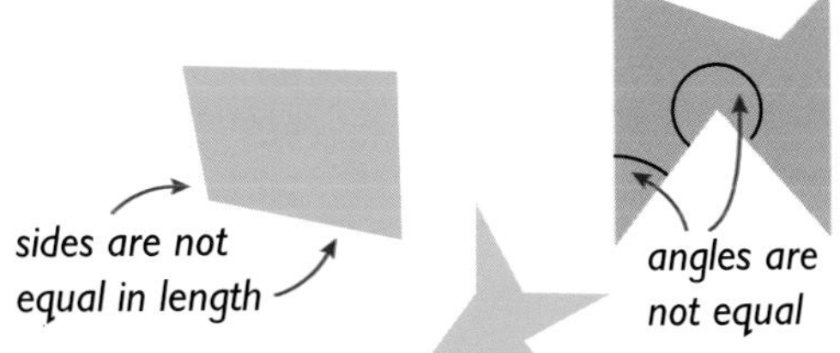

All these 2-D shapes are irregular.

All these 3-D shapes are irregular.

isosceles triangle

See also: triangle

An isosceles triangle has two sides the same length and two angles the same size. Isosceles comes from the Greek words for 'equal legs'.

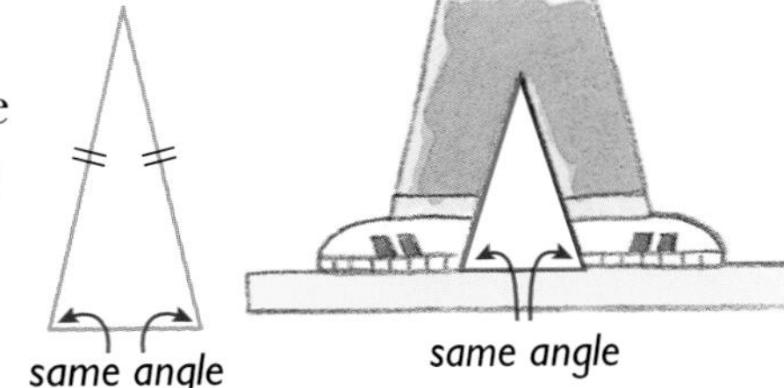

kilogram

See also: mass, metric

A kilogram (kg) is a **metric** unit used for measuring **mass**. One kilogram is equal to one thousand grams (g). One kilogram is approximately 2·2 pounds.

kilometre

See also: distance, length, metric

A kilometre (km) is a **metric** unit we use to measure **length** and **distance**. One kilometre is equal to one thousand metres (m). One kilometre is approximately 0·6 miles.

'Kilo' comes from the Greek work *khilioi* and means one thousand.

A B C D E F G H I J K L M N O P Q R S T U V W X Y Z

kite

See also: adjacent, quadrilateral

A kite is a **quadrilateral** with two pairs of **adjacent** sides of equal length.

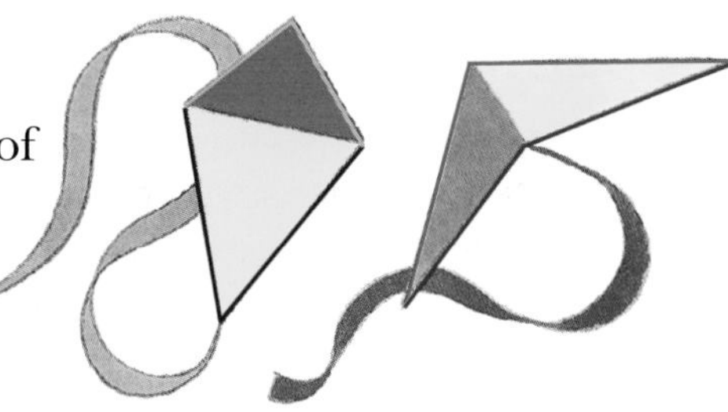

length

See also: distance

The length of a line or object is the **distance** along the line or object from one end to the other. The skipping rope shown is about 1 metre in length, even though its handles are only 50 centimetres apart.

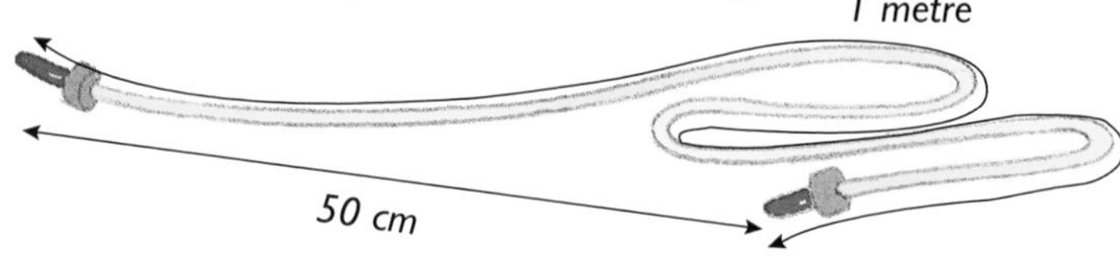

line graph

See also: continuous data

A line graph uses lines to join up points on a graph. They are used with **continuous data** like weight or temperature and are often used to show changes over time.

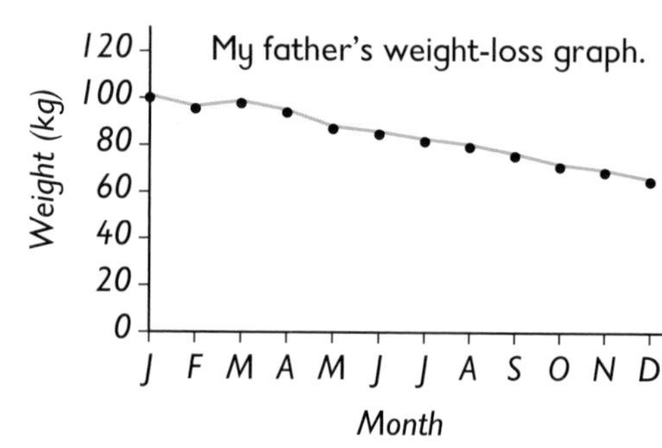

line of symmetry

See also: reflective symmetry

A line of symmetry divides a shape into two reflected halves. If we fold a shape along a line of symmetry one half will cover the other half exactly. The line of symmetry is also known as the mirror line.

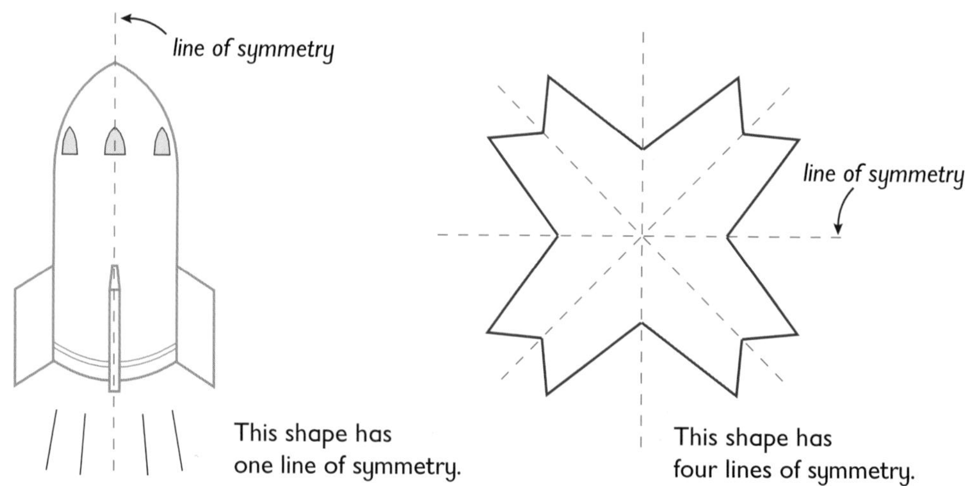

This shape has one line of symmetry.

This shape has four lines of symmetry.

litre

See also: capacity, metric, volume

A litre (l) is a **metric** unit we use to measure **volume** and **capacity**. One litre is equal to one thousand millilitres (ml) and 1·75 pints is approximately one litre.

lowest common multiple

See also: multiple

The lowest common multiple (LCM) of 2, 3 and 4 is 12 because 12 is the lowest number that 2, 3 and 4 will all divide into exactly.

mass

See also: imperial, metric, weight

The mass of an object is the amount of matter it is made from. People often use the word **weight** when they really mean mass. Mass is different from weight. If you went on a space flight you would weigh less than on Earth but your mass would stay the same because your body would not have changed! In the **metric** system, mass is measured in grams (g) and kilograms (kg); in the **imperial** system it is measured in ounces (oz), pounds (lb) and stones (st).

mean

See average

median

See average

metre

See also: distance, length, metric

A metre (m) is a **metric** unit we use to measure **length** and **distance**. One metre is equal to one hundred centimetres (cm), and one thousand metres are equal to one kilometre (km). One metre is slightly longer than one yard.

A B C D E F G H I J K L M N O P Q R S T U V W X Y Z

metric system

See also: imperial units

The metric system is a system of weights and measures that was first used in France in the 1700s and is now used throughout Europe and other parts of the world. Metric units are based on the number ten and powers of ten (10^2, 10^3, and so on). They include metres (m), litres (l) and kilograms (kg).

millennium

A millennium is a period of time that is one thousand years long.

millilitre

See also: capacity, metric, volume

A millilitre (ml) is a **metric** unit used to measure **capacity** and **volume**.
One thousand millilitres is equal to one litre (l). One millilitre of liquid takes up one cubic centimetre (cm^3).

millimetre

See also: distance, length, metric

A millimetre (mm) is a **metric** unit used for measuring **length** and **distance**.
Ten millimetres are equal to one centimetre (cm), and one thousand millimetres equal one metre (m).

'Milli' means one thousandth and comes from the Latin word *mille* meaning one thousand.

minus

See also: negative number, subtraction
Related words: subtract, take away

Minus means 'take away' or subtract and is shown by this sign –. Sometimes we talk about 'minus' or **negative numbers** like –3 and –10.

mixed number

See also: fraction, whole number

A mixed number such as $3\frac{1}{2}$ contains a **whole number** (3) and a **fraction** ($\frac{1}{2}$). It can also be a negative number like $-2\frac{1}{4}$.

mode

See average

multiple

See also: factor, lowest common multiple, product

A multiple is a number that is in a times table. Multiples of three are 3, 6, 9, 12, 15, 18, 21, 24, 27, 30, 33, 36, 39 and they carry on and on in threes. Multiples of ten go up in tens and include 10, 20, 30 … 110 … 360 … 650 and so on. When we multiply two numbers together the answer is a multiple of both the numbers.

multiplication

See also: division
Related word: multiply

Multiplication is a quick way of adding lots of the same number. Instead of adding 6 + 6 + 6 + 6 + 6 we can say 'five lots of six' or 'five times six' and we can write 5 × 6.

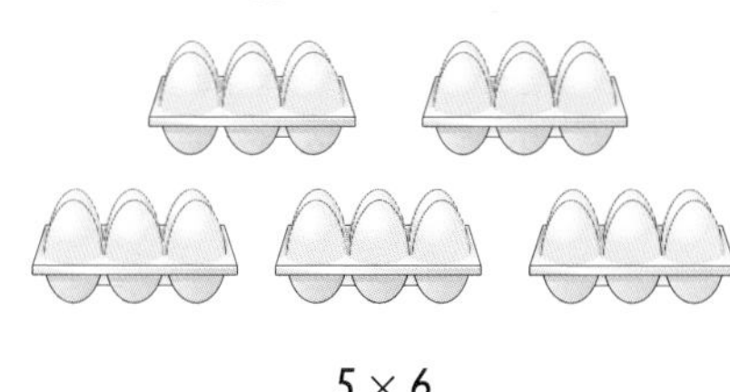

natural number

See also: integer, negative number

Natural numbers is another name for counting numbers, starting with 1. The natural numbers are 1, 2, 3, 4, 5, 6 and so on.

negative number

See also: integer, natural number, positive number

Negative numbers are numbers less than zero. They have a minus sign in front of them, like –6 and –3, to show how many less than zero they are. The number –6 is smaller than –3 because it is 6 less than zero whereas –3 is only 3 less than zero.

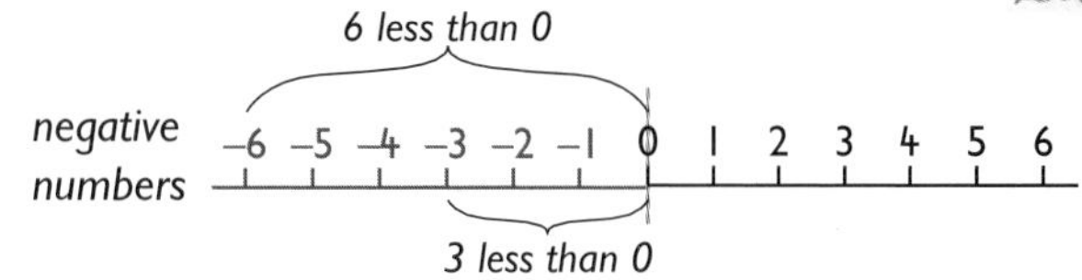

net

See also: tessellation

The net of a three-dimensional object is the two-dimensional shape on paper that we can cut out and fold to make the three-dimensional object. If you open out a cereal box so it is flat (by cutting open some of the edges) you have the net of the box.

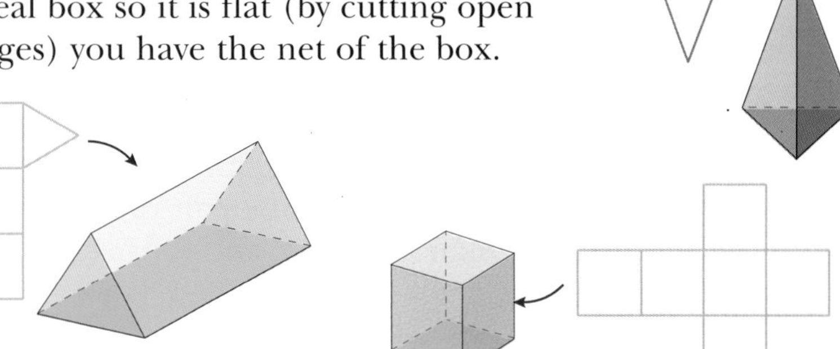

A B C D E F G H I J K L M N O P Q R S T U V W X Y Z

nonagon

A nonagon is a two-dimensional shape with nine straight sides and nine angles.

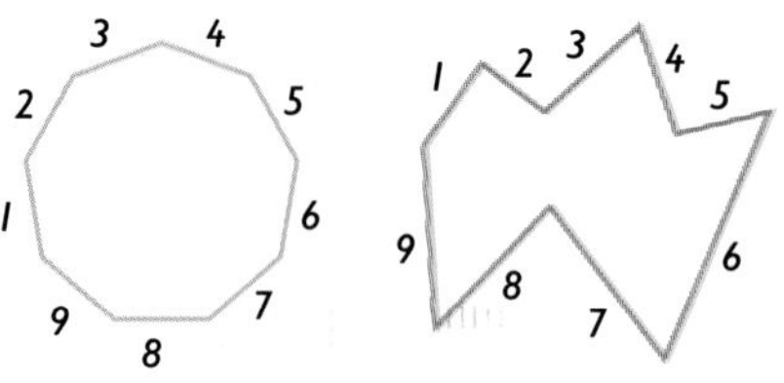

number

See also: decimal, fraction, integer, mixed number, natural number, negative number, symbol

A number is a **symbol** or group of symbols that show how many we have of something. It can also show the position of something in an order. There are different types of numbers, such as **negative numbers**, **natural numbers**, **integers**, **mixed numbers**, **fractions** and **decimals**. Some numbers can belong to more than one type of number. Here are some different numbers: 3 (integer, natural number), $-2\frac{1}{4}$ (mixed number, negative number), 0.43, 37.6 (decimal) and $\frac{1}{2}$ (fraction).

number line

A number line arranges numbers in order on a scale. A ruler is a kind of number line. Number lines can include fractions and negative numbers.

0 10 20 30 40 50 60 70 80 90 100

0 $\frac{1}{4}$ $\frac{1}{2}$ $\frac{3}{4}$ 1

−4 −3 −2 −1 0 1 2 3 4

0 0.5 1.0 1.5 2.0 2.5 3.0 3.5

numeral

Numerals are symbols we use to write numbers, so 5 and 354 are numerals. A picture with three dots on it to stand for 3 is also a numeral.

numerator

See also: denominator, fraction

The numerator is the top number in a **fraction** and shows us how many parts of something we have. In the fraction $\frac{1}{2}$ the numerator is 1 and means 1 out of 2 equal parts.

oblong

See also: rectangle

An oblong is another name for a **rectangle** which has one pair of sides longer than the other, and four right angles.

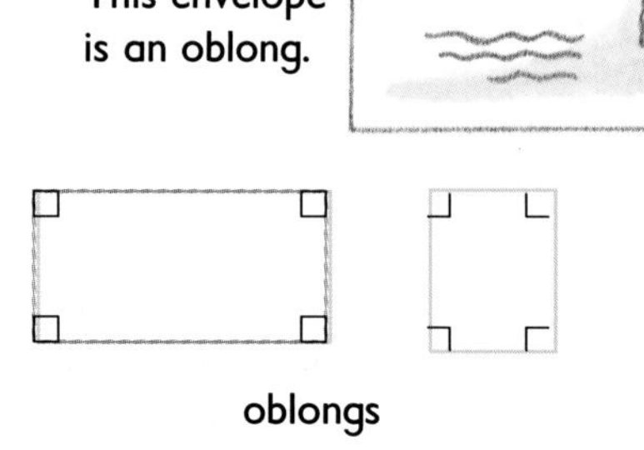

This envelope is an oblong.

oblongs

obtuse angle

See also: acute angle, angle, turn

An obtuse angle is a **turn** that is greater than 90° (90 degrees) but less than 180°.

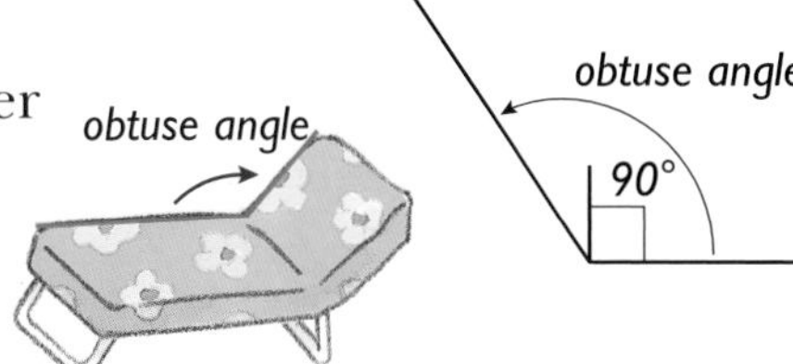

octagon

Related word: octagonal

An octagon is a two-dimensional shape with eight straight sides and eight angles.

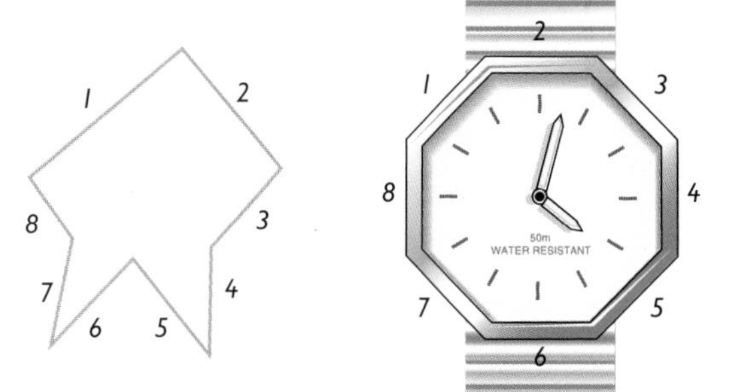

octahedron

An octahedron is a three-dimensional shape with eight faces.

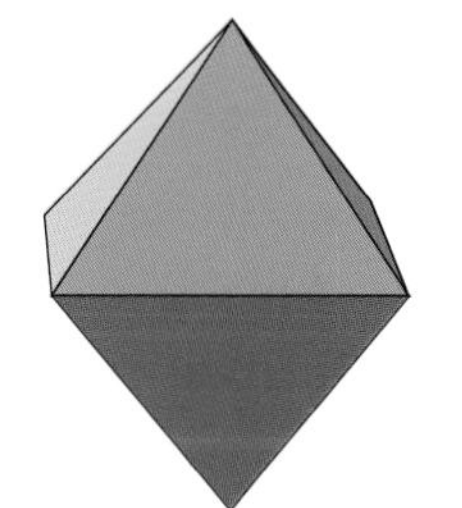

Octagon and octahedron come from the Greek word *octo* meaning eight.

odd number

See also: even number, whole number

Odd numbers are **whole numbers** that cannot be divided exactly by 2 to give whole numbers.
All numbers that end in 1, 3, 5, 7 and 9 are odd.

operation

See also: addition, division, multiplication, subtraction, transformation

An operation is a process of doing something to numbers or shapes. **Addition**, **subtraction**, **multiplication**, **division** and **transformations** are all operations.

order of rotational symmetry

See also: rotational symmetry

The order of rotational symmetry of a shape is the number of different ways the shape will fit into its outline when it is turned.

This shape will fit into its outline four times. It has an order of rotational symmetry of 4.

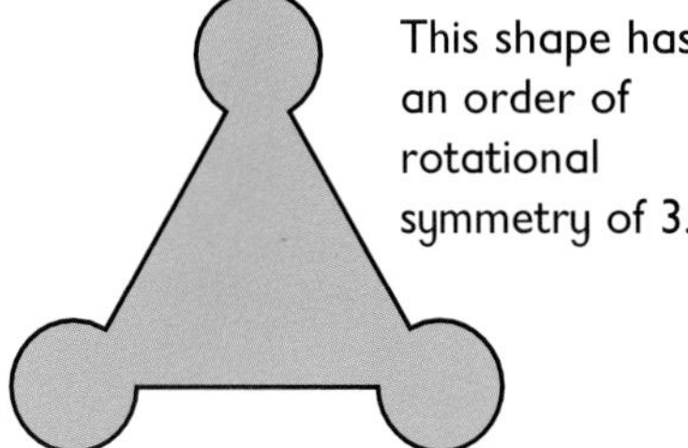

This shape has an order of rotational symmetry of 3.

A B C D E F G H I J K L M N O P Q R S T U V W X Y Z

ordered pair

See also: coordinates

A set of two numbers in which the order is important is called an ordered pair. **Coordinates** are ordered pairs because (5,2) is not the same as (2,5).

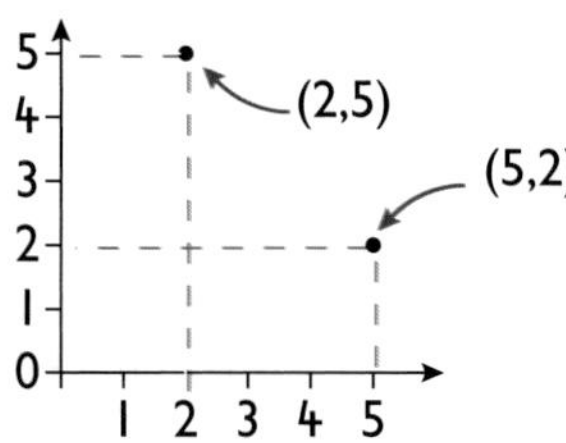

origin

See also: axis, coordinates, graph

The origin of a **graph** is the point where the **axes** meet. The **coordinates** for this point are (0, 0).

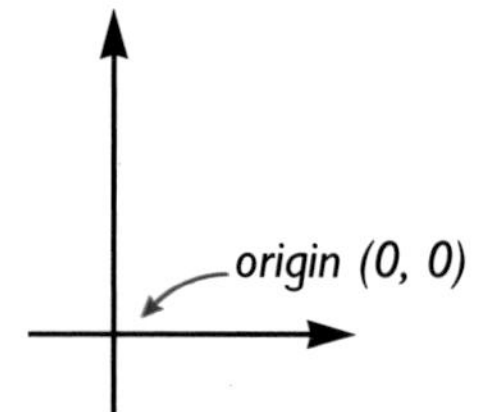

ounce

See also: imperial, mass

An ounce (oz) is an **imperial** unit for measuring **mass**. Sixteen ounces are equal to one pound (lb). Twenty-eight grams (g) is approximately one ounce.

outcome

See also: equally likely outcomes, fair, probability

An outcome is a possible result of doing something. There are six possible outcomes of rolling a dice, all of which are **equally likely** if the dice is **fair**. Throwing a 'three' is one possible outcome.

oval

Related word: ovoid

An oval is a curved two-dimensional shape like the cross-section of an egg.

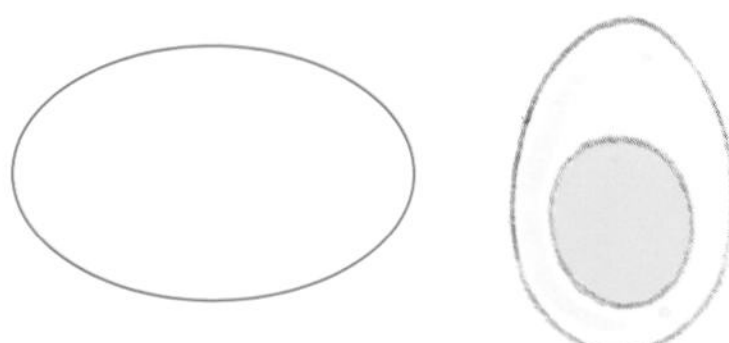

These are both ovals.

pace

See also: length, rate, speed

Pace has two meanings in maths.

a) A pace is an old unit for measuring **length**. It is the distance from the back of one heel to the back of the other when walking.

b) Pace is the **speed** or **rate** at which something is done.

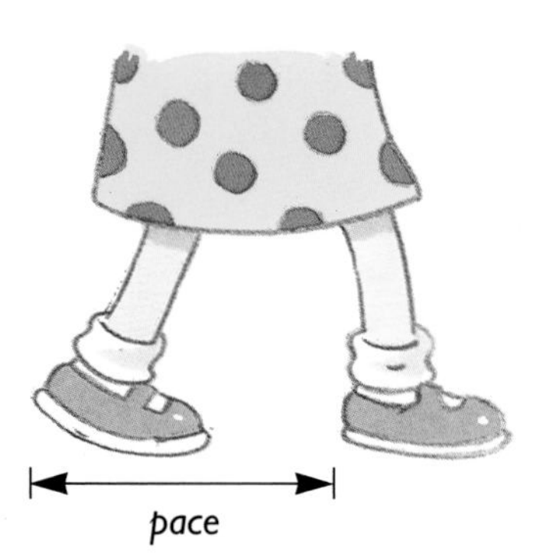

palm

See also: length, span

A palm is an old unit for measuring **length**. It is the distance across a hand with the fingers closed.

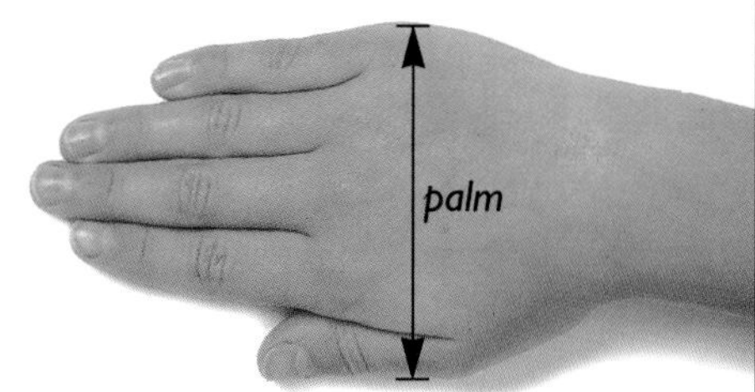

parallel

Parallel lines stay the same distance apart along their whole length. They can be straight or curved and they do not need to be the same length as each other. No matter how long the lines are they will never meet. The symbol ⪢ is sometimes used to show parallel lines.

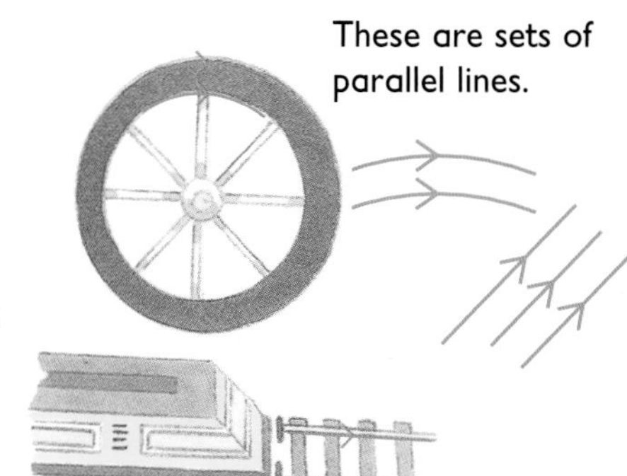
These are sets of parallel lines.

parallelogram

See also: parallel, quadrilateral

A parallelogram is a four-sided two-dimensional shape. Each pair of opposite sides are **parallel** and opposite angles are equal .

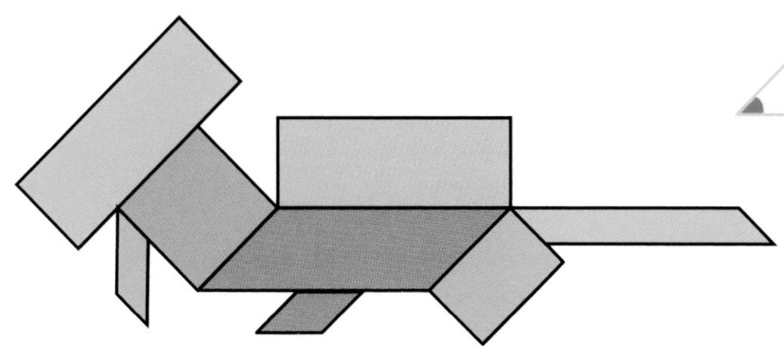
This pattern is made from parallelograms.

Pairs of opposite angles are the same and pairs of opposite sides are parallel and the same length.

pentagon

Related word: pentagonal

A pentagon is a two-dimensional shape with five straight sides and five angles. A regular pentagon has all its sides the same length and all its angles equal.

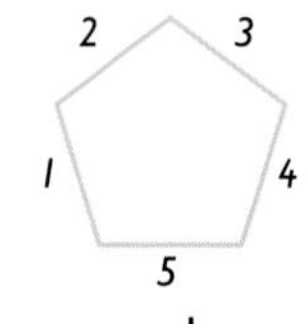

regular pentagon

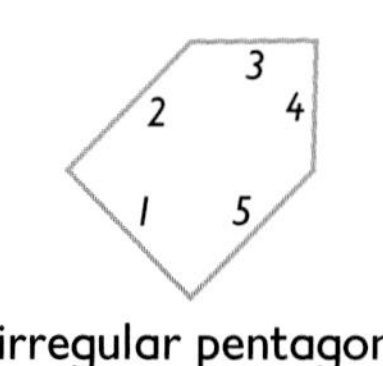

irregular pentagons

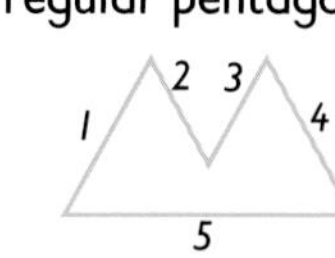

A B C D E F G H I J K L M N O P Q R S T U V W X Y Z

percentage

Related word: per cent

A percentage is a special fraction which has a denominator of 100, like $\frac{67}{100}$ or $\frac{8}{100}$. We write $\frac{67}{100}$ as 67% and $\frac{8}{100}$ as 8%. We say 8% as 'eight per cent'. Per cent means 'for every hundred'.

Percentages help us to compare things. For example, Sam's three test results of $\frac{9}{15}$, $\frac{21}{35}$ and $\frac{15}{20}$ can be turned into percentages to compare them.

$$\frac{9}{15} = \frac{3}{5} = \frac{60}{100} = 60\%$$
$$\frac{21}{35} = \frac{3}{5} = \frac{60}{100} = 60\%$$
$$\frac{15}{20} = \frac{3}{4} = \frac{75}{100} = 75\%$$

In the first two tests he achieved 60% but he did better in the third test, getting 75%.

perimeter

See also: circumference, distance, length

The perimeter of a shape is the **distance** all round it. It is a measure of **length** and is measured in centimetres, metres or some other unit of length.
The perimeter of a circle is called the **circumference**.

The perimeter of the lawn is 16 metres.

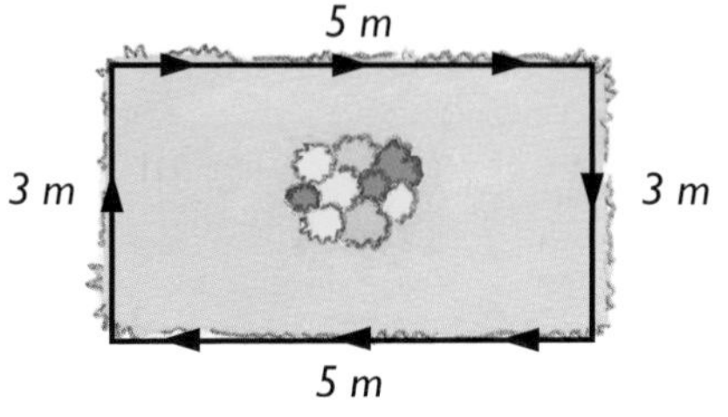

perpendicular

See also: right-angle

A perpendicular line is a line that is drawn at a **right-angle** (90°) to another line.

The blue line is perpendicular to the red line.

The nail is perpendicular to the wall.

pi

See also: circumference, diameter

For all circles, the **circumference** divided by the **diameter** always gives the same number, $\frac{22}{7}$ (approximately 3·14). This number is called pi and has the symbol π. Pi is special because it shows the relationship between the circumference and diameter for every circle.

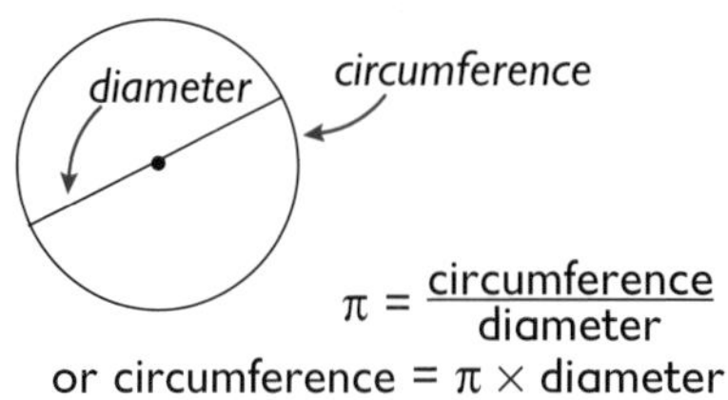

$$\pi = \frac{\text{circumference}}{\text{diameter}}$$

or circumference = π × diameter

This means, for any circle we can calculate the circumference if we know the diameter, or we can calculate the diameter if we know the circumference.

circumference
$= \pi \times$ diameter
$= \frac{22}{7} \times 14$ cm
$= 44$ cm

pictogram

A pictogram is a type of graph that uses pictures to show information.

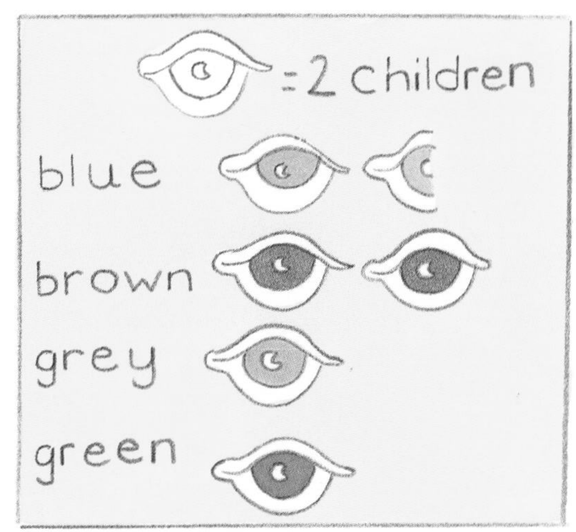

A pictogram showing eye colours of some children in a class.

pie graph, pie chart

See also: sector

A pie graph (also called a pie chart) looks like a round pie cut into slices. It is a type of graph which divides a circle into slices or **sectors** of different sizes to show different amounts.

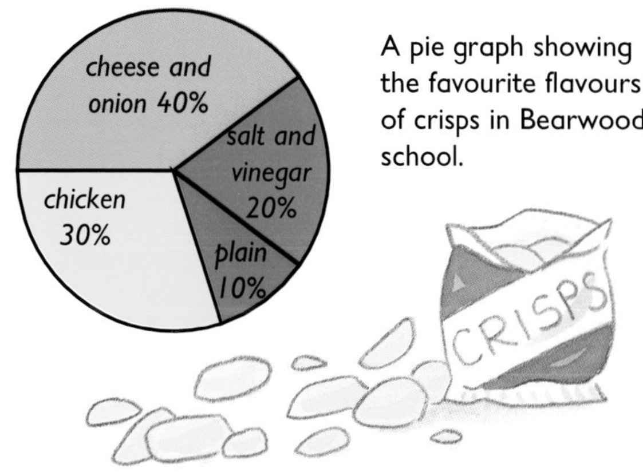

A pie graph showing the favourite flavours of crisps in Bearwood school.

pint

See also: capacity, imperial, volume

Pint is an **imperial** unit for measuring **capacity** and **volume**. Eight pints are equal to one gallon (gall). One pint is a little more than $\frac{1}{2}$ litre.

place value

Place value means that the position of a digit in a number shows how much it is worth. The two in 25 is worth twenty, the two in 2784 is worth two thousand and the two in 14·23 is worth two-tenths.

Th	H	T	U	t	h
		2	5		
2	7	8	4		
		1	4	2	3

A B C D E F G H I J K L M N O P Q R S T U V W X Y Z

plane

See also: dimension, face

A plane is a flat surface. We can create a plane by cutting straight through a three-dimensional object, like a pack of butter or a tree. A plane shape is a flat, two-dimensional shape like a triangle or square.

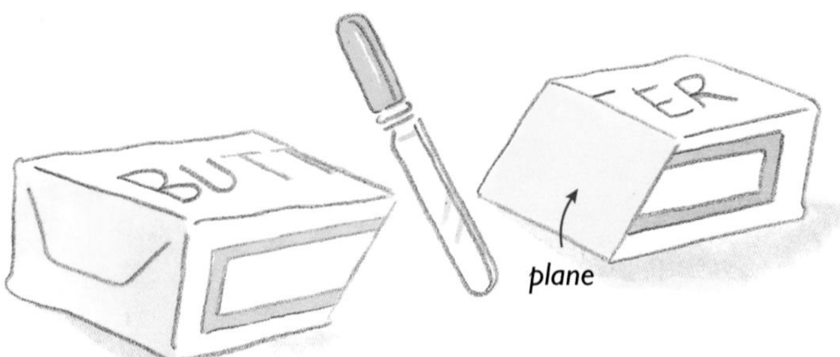

plane shapes

plus

See also: addition, subtraction, symbol

Plus means **add** and uses the symbol +.

p.m.

See also: a.m., twenty-four-hour clock

The abbreviation p.m. stands for *post meridiem.* It is used to show the time between midday (noon) and midnight on the twelve-hour clock.

polygon

See also: irregular shape, regular polygon, two-dimensional

A polygon is a **two-dimensional** shape that has sides made from straight lines. Triangles, squares and hexagons are examples of polygons.

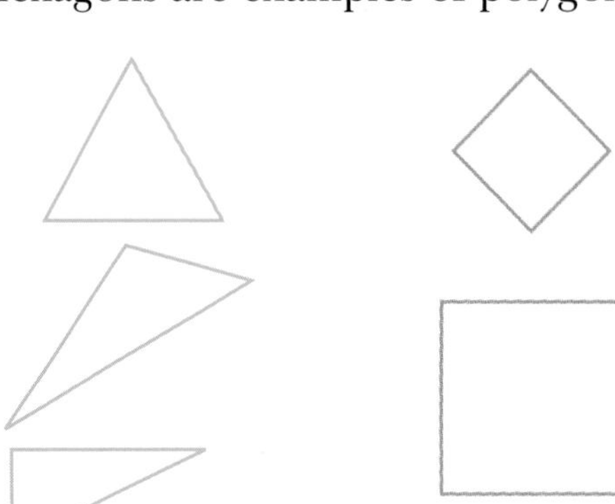

triangles squares hexagons

polyhedron

See also: irregular shape, regular polyhedron, three-dimensional

A polyhedron (plural polyhedra) is a **three-dimensional** shape with flat faces. Cubes, cuboids and triangular prisms are examples of polyhedra.

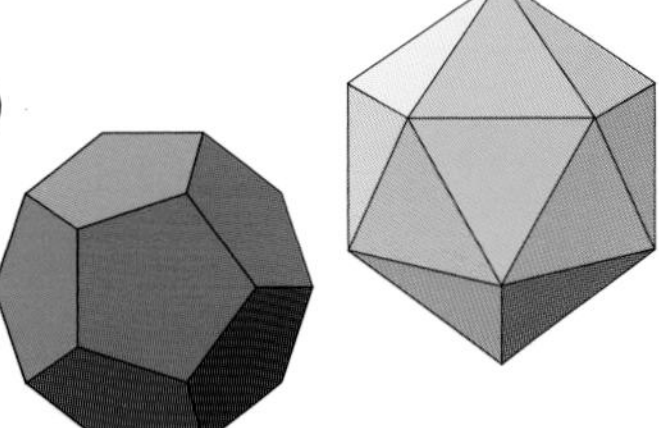

dodecahedron icosahedron

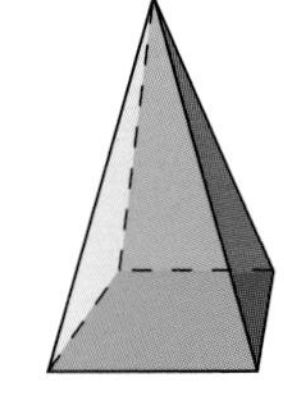

square pyramid

Poly is a Greek word meaning 'many'; polygon means 'many angles' and polyhedron means 'many faces'.

positive number

See also: integer, natural number, negative number

Positive numbers are numbers which are larger than zero, like 3, $56\frac{1}{2}$ and 0·42.

possible

See also: outcome, probability, unlikely

We say things are possible if they have a chance of happening. When we roll a dice it is possible to get a 'six'. We buy lottery tickets because it is possible we might win.

pound

See also: imperial, mass

Pound has two meanings in maths.

a) Pound can mean a unit of money written using the symbol £. One pound is equal to 100 pence.

b) Pound is also an **imperial** unit for measuring **mass**. It has the symbol lb. One pound is equal to sixteen ounces (oz); one pound is a little less than half a kilogram.

This new baby weighs 7.5 pounds.

power

See also: cube, square

The power of a number shows how many of the same number are multiplied together. For example, 2^3 means 'two to the power three', 2 cubed, or $2 \times 2 \times 2$, which equals 8.

prime factor

See also: factor, prime number

Prime factors of a number are **factors** that are also **prime numbers**, that is, they have only themselves and 1 as factors. The prime factors of 12 are 2 and 3.

A B C D E F G H I J K L M N O **P** Q R S T U V W X Y Z

prime number

See also: factor, whole number

A prime number is a whole number that only has two **factors**, itself and 1. The numbers 2, 3, 5, 7, 11 and 13 are some prime numbers, but 1 is not a prime number because it only has one factor.

prism

See also: cuboid, cylinder, triangular prism

A prism is a three-dimensional shape that has the same cross-section all along its length. **Cuboids**, **cylinders** and **triangular prisms** are all prisms.

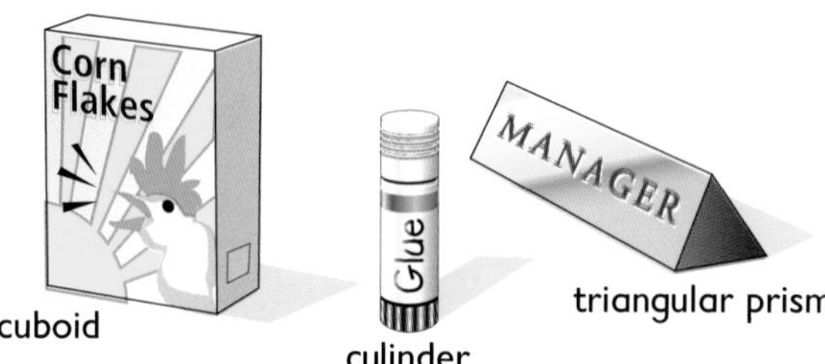

probability

See also: certain, equally likely outcomes, fair, impossible, outcome, unlikely

Probability is about the chance, or likelihood, of something happening. When we toss a **fair** coin we have an even or equal chance of throwing heads or tails. So the probability of getting a 'head' is one out of two or $\frac{1}{2}$. When we roll a fair dice the probability of getting a 'five' is one out of six or $\frac{1}{6}$.

probability of heads = $\frac{1}{2}$ (0.5)

probability scale

See also: certain, impossible, possible, probability, scale

A probability scale is used to measure **probability** on a **scale** marked from zero to one. The zero means there is no chance of something happening, it is **impossible**. The probability of Friday being the day after Sunday is zero. When something is **certain** to happen, like night following day, we say it has a probability of one. Other events, like the chance of it raining today, are **possible**, and so have probabilities between these two extremes. If two outcomes are equally likely, we say they have an even chance of occurring, or a probability of a half.

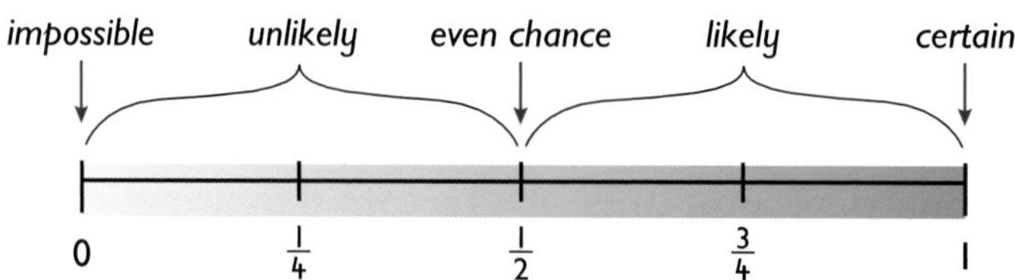

product

See also: multiply

The product of two numbers is the answer when we **multiply** them together. The product of 3 and 4 is 12.

proper fraction

See also: improper fraction,

A proper fraction has a numerator (top number) that is smaller than the denominator (bottom number), like $\frac{1}{6}$ and $\frac{3}{4}$. It is also called a common fraction or a vulgar fraction.

proportion

See ratio

protractor

See also: angle, angle measurer, degree

A protractor is a type of **angle measurer**, used for finding how many **degrees** are in an **angle**.

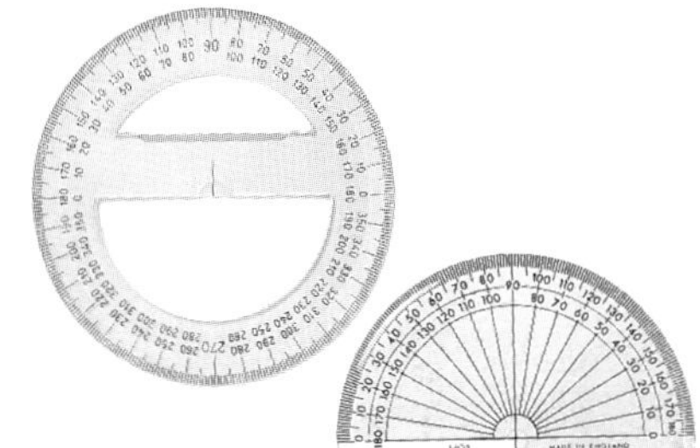

pyramid

See also: vertex

A pyramid is a three-dimensional shape which has a polygon for its base and triangular faces which meet at one **vertex**.

The famous Egyptian pyramids are examples of pyramids which have a square as their base.

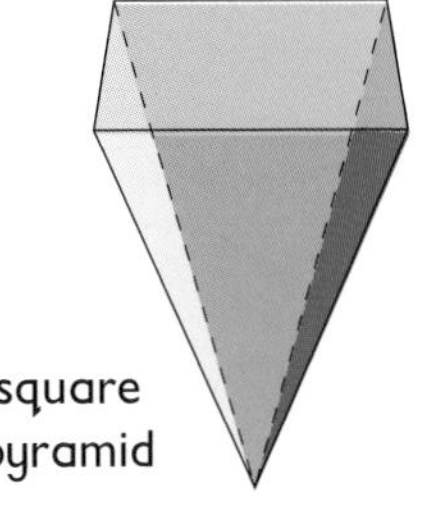

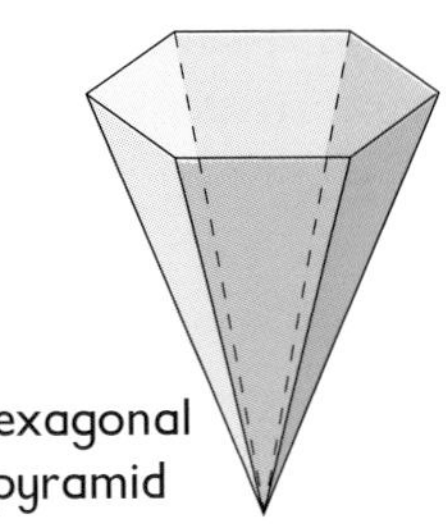

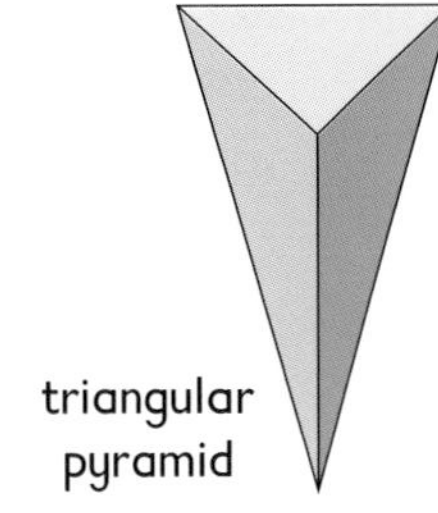

quadrant

See also: sector

A quadrant is a special **sector** that is one quarter of a circle.

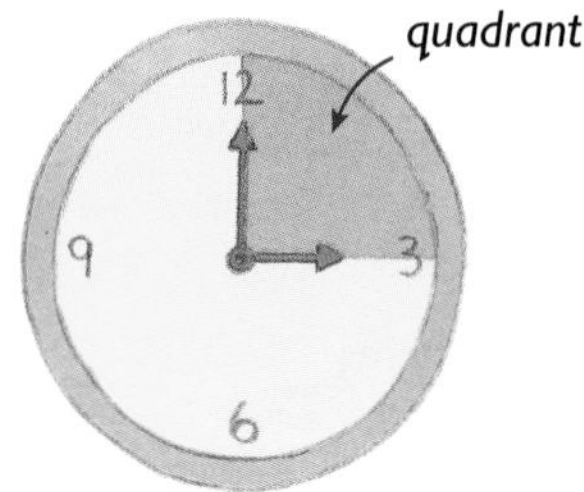

quadrilateral

See also: kite, parallelogram, rectangle, rhombus, square, trapezium

A quadrilateral is any two-dimensional shape with four straight sides. These shapes are all types of quadrilaterals: **square**, **rectangle**, **rhombus**, **trapezium**, **parallelogram** and **kite**.

All these shapes are quadrilaterals.

quart

See also: capacity, imperial, volume

A quart is an **imperial** unit for measuring **volume** and **capacity**. Four quarts are equal to one gallon (gall). One quart is approximately 1·1 litres (l).

quarter

A quarter is one part of something that has been divided into four equal parts. It can be written as a fraction ($\frac{1}{4}$), a decimal (0·25) or a percentage (25%).

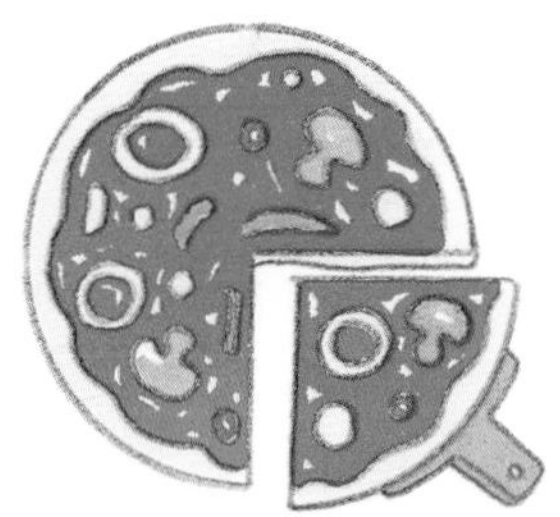

This slice is one quarter of the pizza.

quarter turn

See also: anticlockwise, clockwise, rotation, turn

A quarter turn is a quarter of a full **rotation clockwise** or **anticlockwise** and measures 90° (90 degrees).

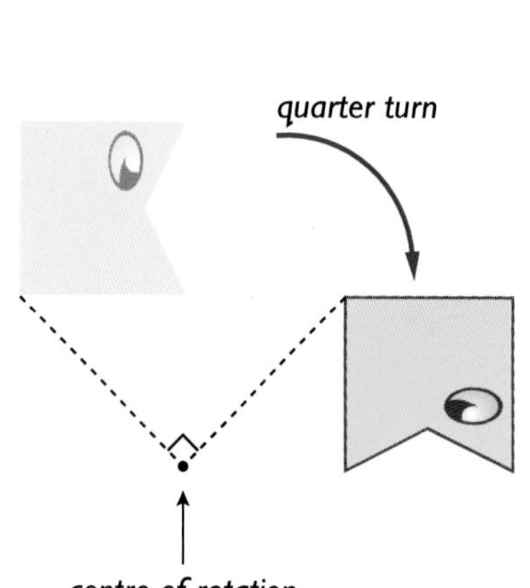

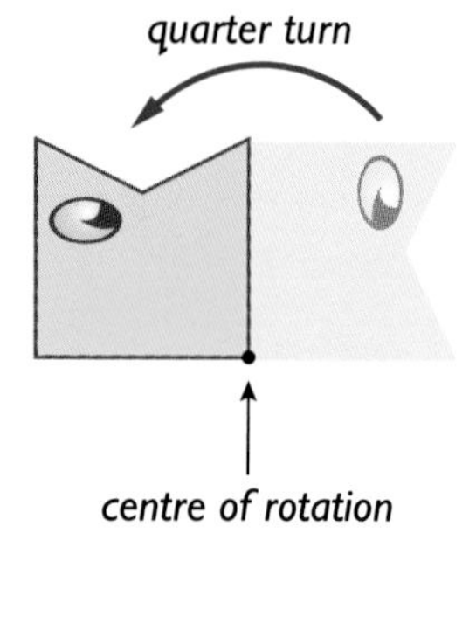

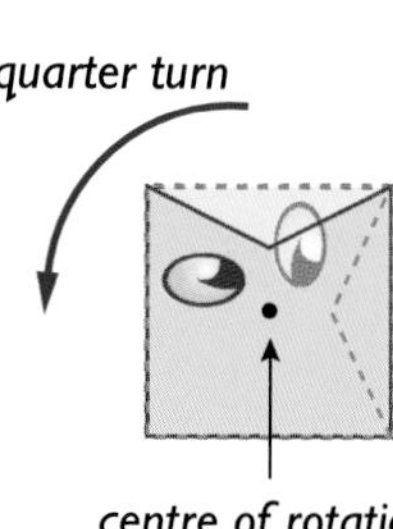

quotient

See also: remainder

The quotient is the whole number part of the answer to a division question. In $12 \div 4 = 3$ the quotient is 3. In $9 \div 2 = 4\ r\ 1$ the quotient is 4 and the **remainder** is 1.

radius

See also: circumference, diameter, pi

The radius of a circle is the distance from the centre to any point on the **circumference**. It is half the **diameter**. The plural of radius is radii.

For any circle the radius = circumference $\div 2\pi$.

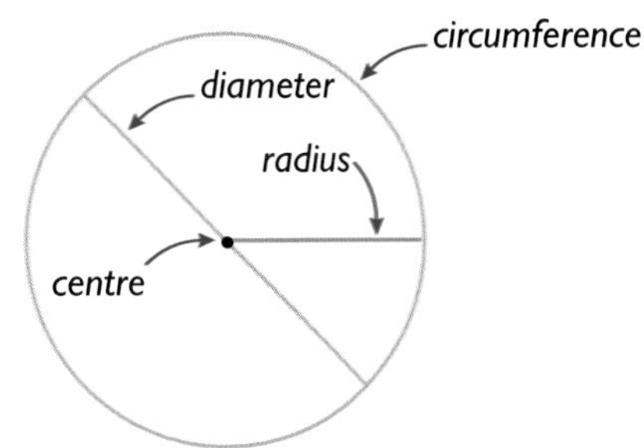

random, random number

See also: bias, equally likely outcomes, fair, probability

Random numbers are numbers that are selected by chance. All numbers within a specified range have an equal chance of occurring. Lottery numbers are selected randomly.

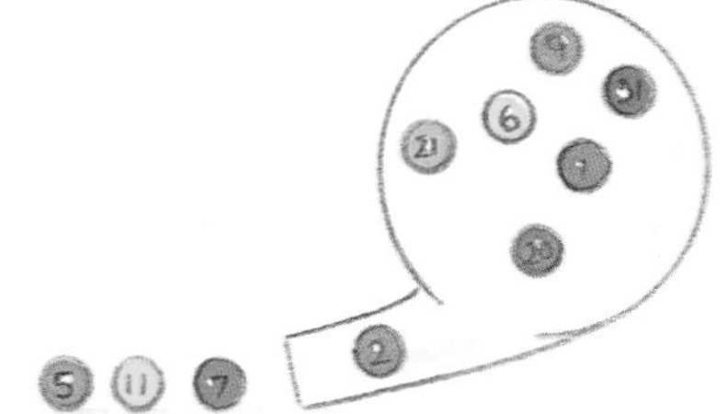

range

The range of a group of numbers is the difference between the highest and lowest values. This set of data shows the number of goals scored in several football matches: 2, 1, 4, 3, 3, 2, 5, 2. The range is from 1 to 5 and equals 4.

rate

See also: speed

Rate is the relationship between two different units of measurement, such as metres and seconds.
We describe one unit in terms of the other and use the word 'per' (symbol /) which means 'for each'. For example, 15 m/s means 15 metres per (or for each) second, £2/kg means £2 per kilogram, 20p/hour means 20p per hour.

A B C D E F G H I J K L M N O P Q R S T U V W X Y Z

ratio

Ratio is the relationship between two quantities. If we use 100 ml of blackcurrant juice and 300 ml of water to make a drink, the ratio would be 100 parts blackcurrant juice to 300 parts water, or 100 : 300 (we use the symbol : to show a ratio). We can also write this as 1 : 3 (or 1 to 3) because 100 : 300 and 1 : 3 are in the same ratio or proportion.

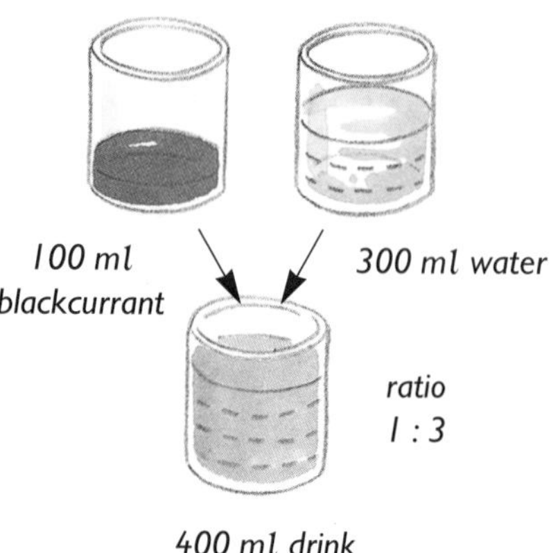

rectangle

See also: oblong, parallel, quadrilateral, right-angle
Related word: rectangular

A rectangle is a four-sided shape with two pairs of **parallel** sides that meet at **right-angles**. A square is a special kind of rectangle because all its sides are the same length.

These are rectangles.

rectangular number

See also: square number, triangular number

A rectangular number can be drawn as a pattern of dots which make a rectangle with more than one equal row. Examples of rectangular numbers are 4, 6, 8, 9, and 10. All even numbers except 2 are rectangular numbers.

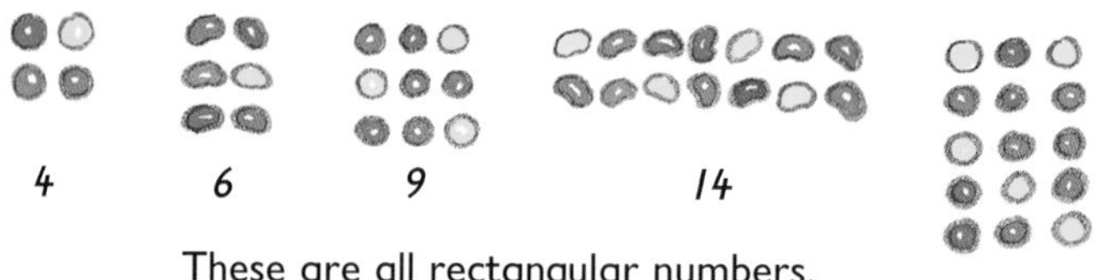

These are all rectangular numbers.

rectangular prism

See also: cube, cuboid, prism, rectangle

A rectangular prism is a three-dimensional shape that has the same sized rectangular faces at each end. The cross-section is the same throughout its length.

recurring decimal

A recurring decimal is one that never ends. It goes on repeating a digit or a set of digits over and over, for example 4·33333… , 0·1666666… , 0·272727… and so on. A dot above the decimal is used to show that digits repeat for ever, for example, $4{\cdot}\dot{3}$ (four point three recurring), $0{\cdot}1\dot{6}$ and $0{\cdot}\dot{2}\dot{7}$.

reflection

See also:
line of symmetry
reflective symmetry,
transformation
Related word:
reflect

A reflection is a way of changing a shape like a mirror does. It is a type of **transformation**. The shape is reflected in the **line of symmetry** (or mirror line).

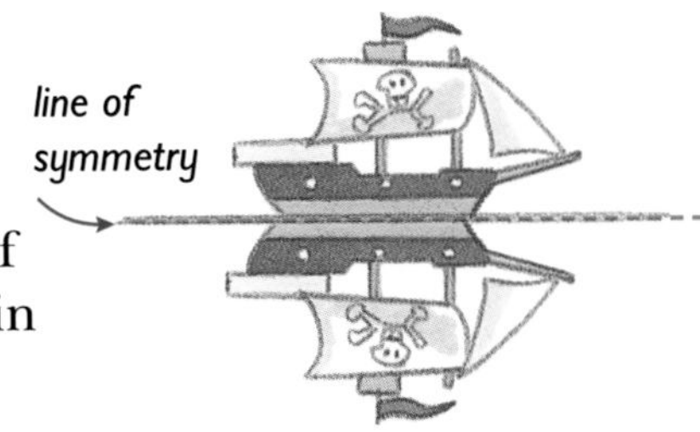

reflective symmetry

See also:
line of symmetry,
rotational symmetry,
symmetry

A two-dimensional shape has reflective symmetry if we can fold it along a straight line so that the two halves fit over each other exactly. This line is called a **line of symmetry**. A three-dimensional shape has reflective symmetry if it can be split into two reflected halves.

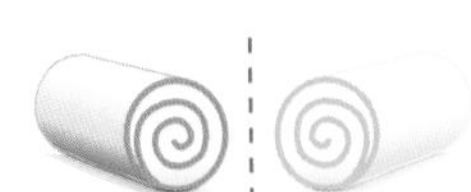

This three-dimensional object has reflective symmetry.

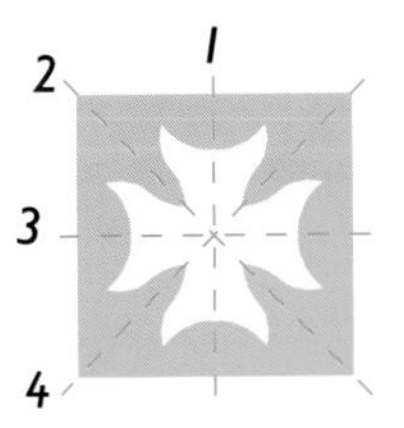

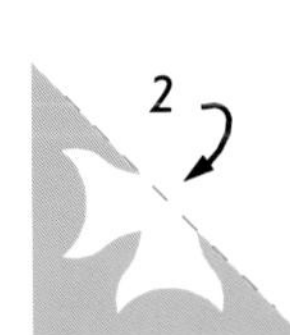

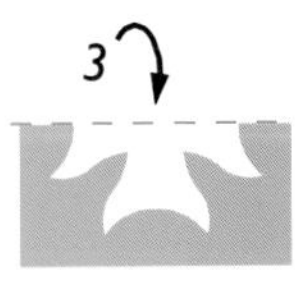

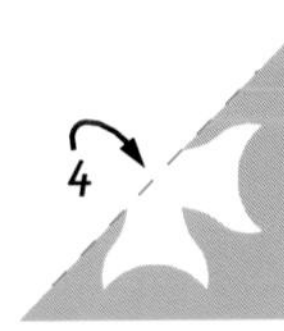

This two-dimensional shape has four lines of reflective symmetry.

reflex angle

See also:
acute angle, angle,
obtuse angle,
straight angle

A reflex angle is more than 180° (180 degrees) but less than 360°.

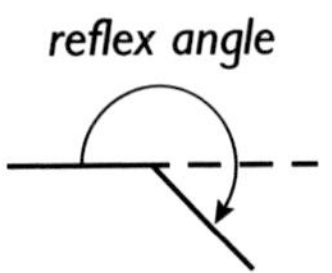

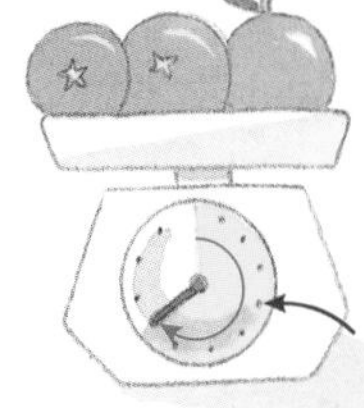

region

See also:
area

A region is a part of a surface. A line of symmetry on a square divides it into two equal regions. A map might show a mountainous region or a desert region.

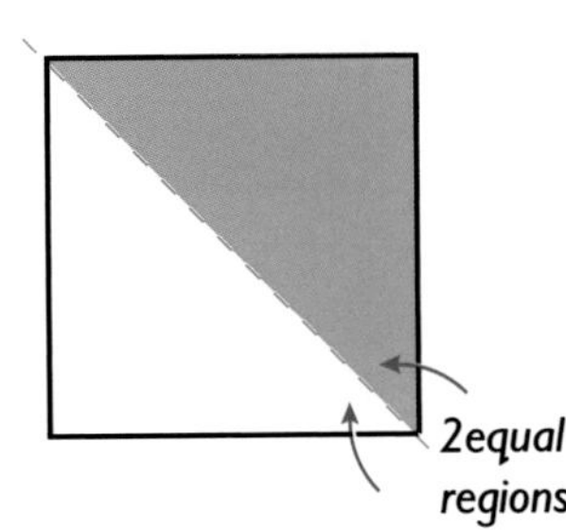

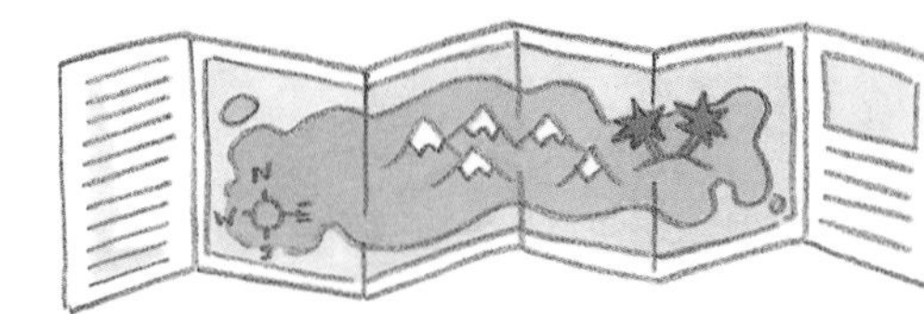

The map shows regions of desert and mountains.

regular polygon

See also: irregular, two-dimensional
Related word: regularity

A regular polygon is a **two-dimensional** shape with all its sides and angles equal.

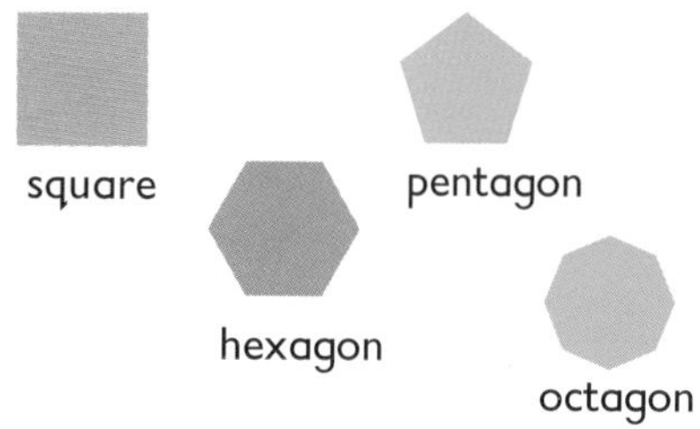

These are regular polygons.

regular polyhedron

See also: cube, dodecahedron, icosahedron, irregular, octahedron, polygon, tetrahedron, three-dimensional
Related word: regularity

A regular polyhedron (plural polyhedra) is a **three-dimensional** shape whose faces are all identical **regular polygons**. The same number of edges meet at each vertex (corner). There are only five types of regular polyhedra: **tetrahedron**, **cube**, **octahedron**, **dodecahedron**, **icosahedron**.

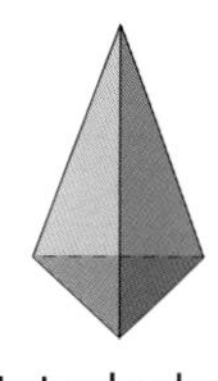
tetrahedron

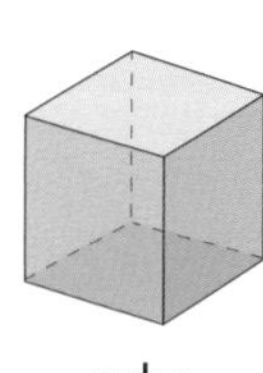
cube

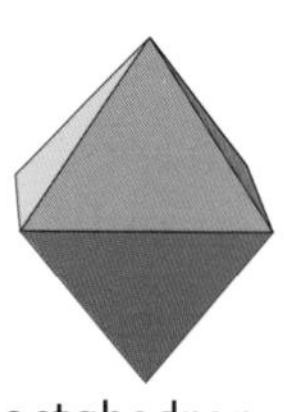
octahedron

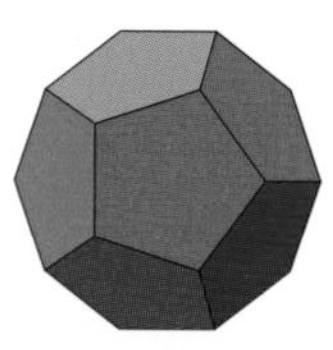
dodecahedron

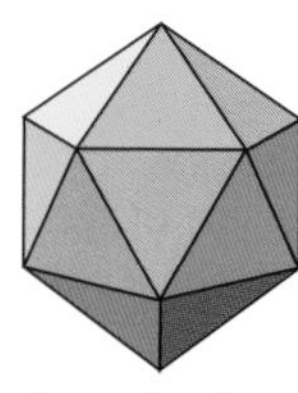
icosahedron

These are all regular polyhedra.

remainder

See also: quotient

The remainder is what is left over after dividing numbers that do not divide exactly. For example, $7 \div 3$ is 2 remainder 1 (or 2 r 1).

rhombus

See also: parallel, parallelogram, quadrilateral, right-angle

A rhombus is a four-sided shape with opposite sides that are **parallel** and all sides are equal in length. It is a special kind of **parallelogram**. A square is a special rhombus that has four **right-angles**.

right-angle

See also: turn

A right-angle is a **turn** of 90° (90 degrees).

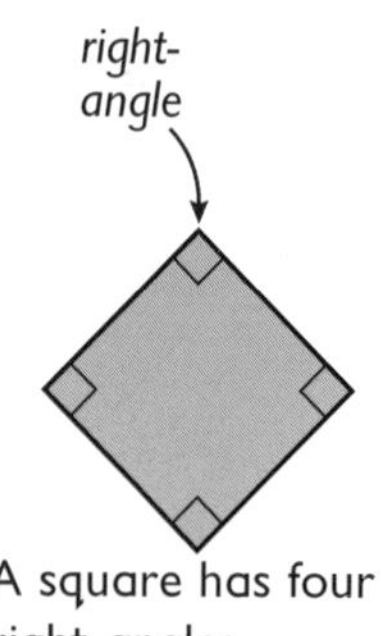

A square has four right-angles.

right-angled triangle

See also: angle, triangle

A right-angled triangle has one **angle** of 90° (90 degrees).

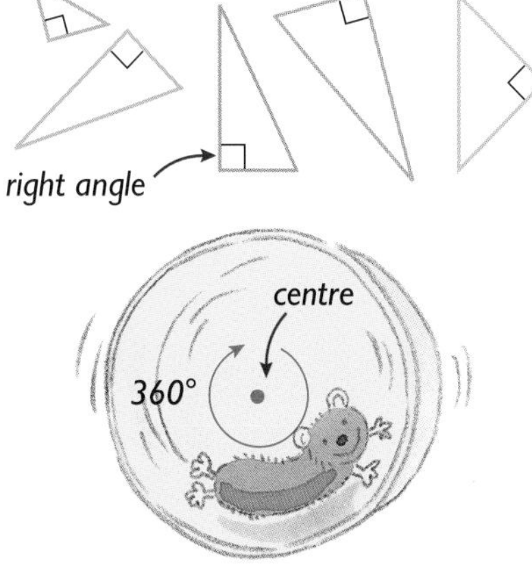

A wheel rotates around its centre.

rotation

See also: centre of rotation, transformation, turn
Related word: rotate

One rotation is a full **turn** and is 360° (360 degrees). In a rotation all the points of a shape turn through the same angle around a point known as the **centre of rotation**. It is a type of **transformation**.

rotational symmetry

See also: order of rotational symmetry, symmetry, turn

A two-dimensional shape has rotational symmetry if it fits into its outline in more than one way as it is turned through a full **turn**. A square fits into its outline in four ways, so it has an order of rotational symmetry of 4. A three-dimensional shape has rotational symmetry when it fits into its 'outline' in more than one way as it is rotated around a central point.

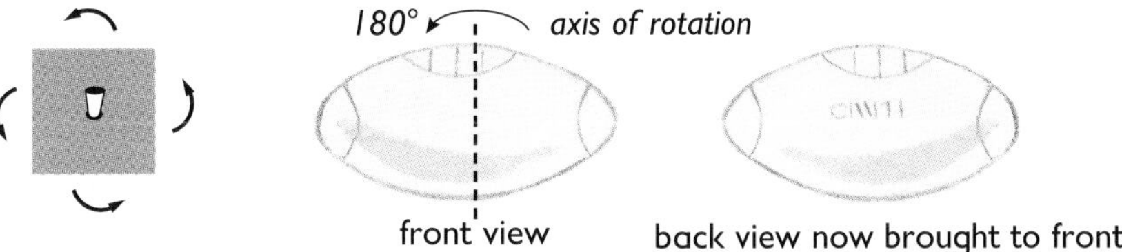

round, round down, round up, rounding

See also: approximation

Rounding is when we round numbers up or down if we want a rough answer or an **approximation**. We usually round numbers to the nearest 10 or 100. For example, to get a rough answer to 52 + 19 we might round 52 to 50 and 19 to 20, giving 50 + 20. With decimal numbers we might round them to the nearest whole number, so 0·7 becomes 1 and 4·25 becomes 4.

scale

See also: enlargement, ratio, scale factor, similar

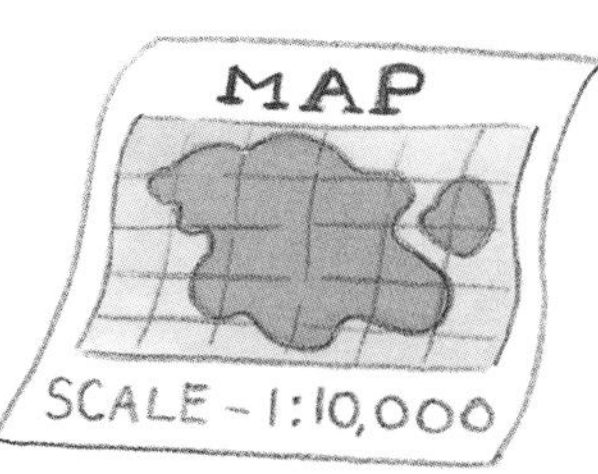

Scale has two meanings in maths.

a) Something made to scale has every part made larger or smaller by the same amount. We use scale in model making, plans and maps. If a map scale is 1 : 10,000, 1 cm on the map stands for 10,000 cm in real life.

b) A scale is a series of evenly spaced marks on something used for measuring. Thermometers, rulers and the axes of graphs have scales.

0 1 2
cm

A B C D E F G H I J K L M N O P Q R S T U V W X Y Z

scale factor

See also: enlargement, ratio, scale, similar

The scale factor is the amount by which something has been made larger or smaller. A square that is enlarged by scale factor 3 has sides that are 3 times longer than on the original square.

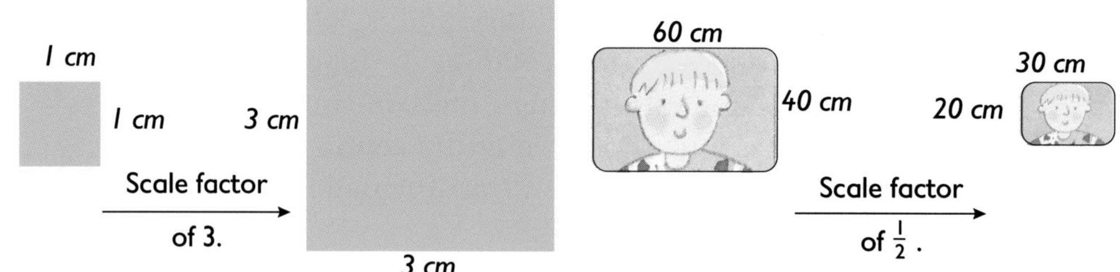

scalene triangle

See also: angle, triangle

A scalene triangle has all its sides of different lengths and all its angles of different sizes.

scales

See also: mass, weight

Scales are used to measure the **mass**, or **weight**, of something. We might use bathroom scales to measure our weight, kitchen scales to measure the weight of things for cooking and balance scales to measure the mass of small objects.

sector

See also: circumference, radius

A sector is like a slice of a circle, such as a piece of pizza. Its edges are the 2 **radii** and the part of the **circumference** (arc) between them.

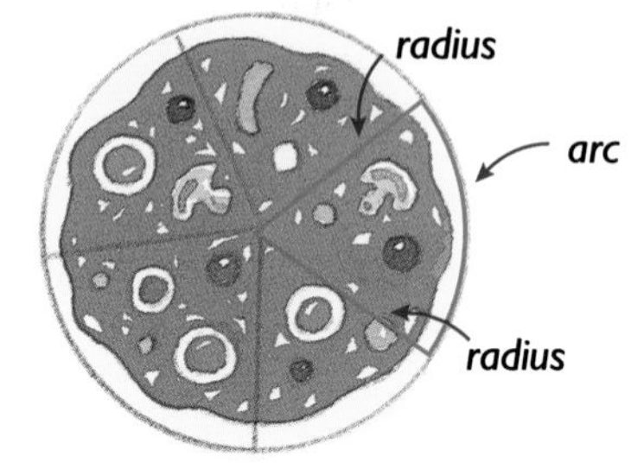

This pizza has five sectors. One of them is highlighted

segment

See also: chord, circumference, semicircle

A segment is a part of something.
A segment of a circle is a piece whose boundaries are a **chord** and part of the **circumference** (arc). A **semicircle** is a type of segment.

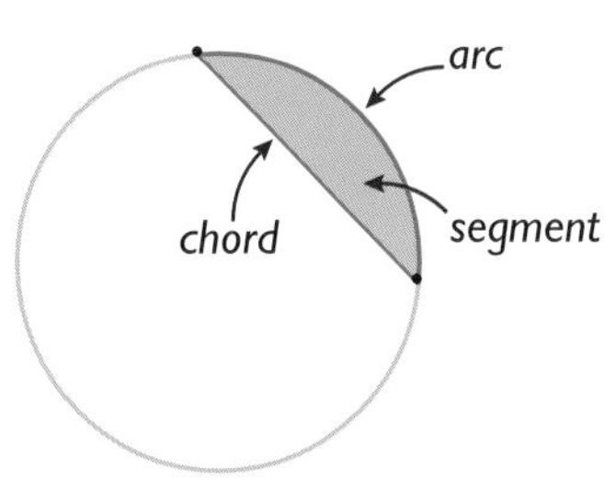

semicircle

A semicircle is half a circle.

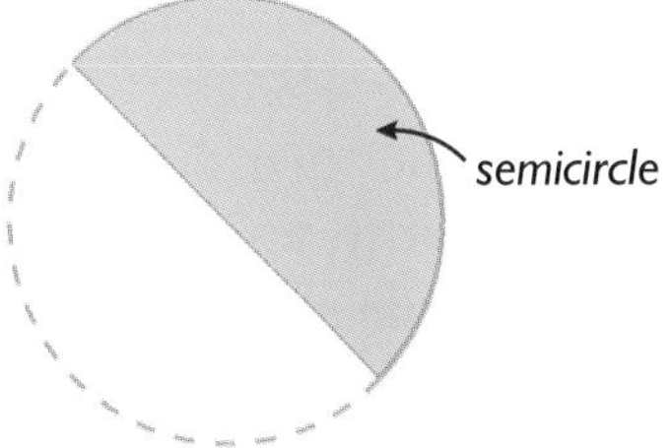

sequence

A sequence is something arranged in a particular order and according to a rule. Number patterns like 2, 4, 6, 8 … and 1, 3, 6, 10 … are sequences because the numbers in each are arranged according to a rule.

set

See also: Carroll diagram, Venn diagram

A set is a group of things. We might have a set of football cards or a tea set. In mathematics we might have a set of even numbers or a set of numbers divisible by 5. We can show sets using **Venn** and **Carroll diagrams**.

sign

See symbol

similar

See also: congruent, ratio, scale, transformation
Related word: similarity

Things that have been made larger or smaller but have not changed their shape are known as similar. Similar objects can be positioned in different directions. Their angles are still the same size and their sides are in the same proportion or **ratio**. Models built to **scale** are similar.

These stars are similar.

A B C D E F G H I J K L M N O P Q R S T U V W X Y Z

sixth

A sixth is one part of something that has been divided into 6 equal parts and is written $\frac{1}{6}$.

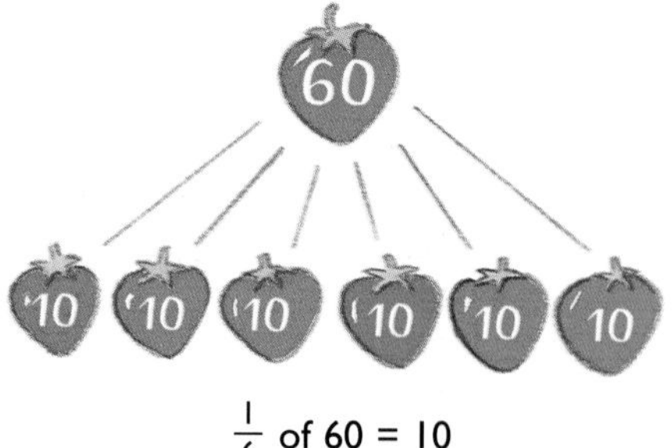

$\frac{1}{6}$ of 60 = 10

solid shape

See also: dimension, plane shape, three-dimensional

Solid shapes are shapes that have three dimensions – length, width and height – and are often called **three-dimensional** shapes. Examples include: cuboid, sphere and cone.

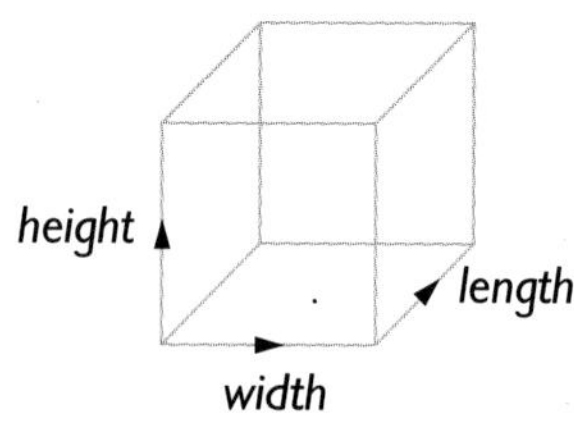

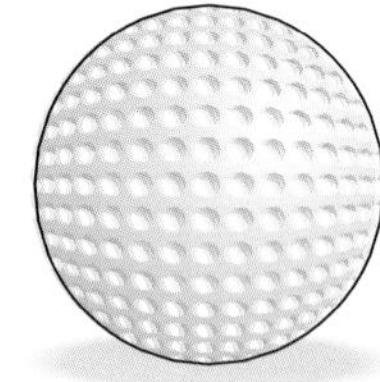

Computer monitors and golf balls are solid shapes.

span

See also: length, palm

A span is an old unit for measuring **length**. It is the distance from the thumb to the tip of the little finger across a hand with the fingers spread.

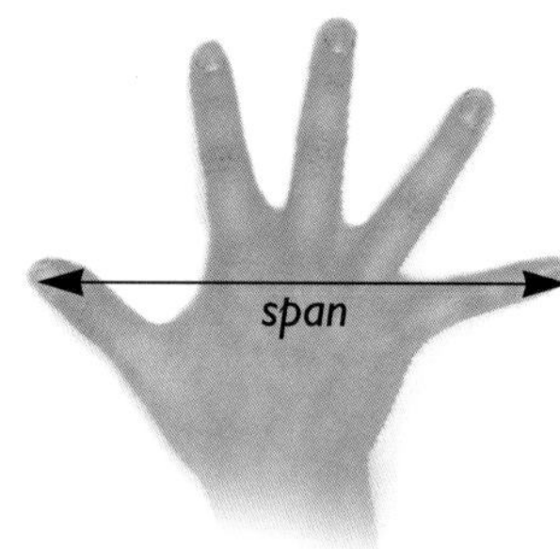

speed

See also: rate

Speed is a measure of how fast something is moving and is usually measured in units of distance (miles, kilometres, metres) per unit of time (hours, minutes, seconds). For example, a car travelling at a speed of 100 kilometres (km) per hour will travel a distance of 100 km in 1 hour.

To find the average speed of something we divide the distance travelled by the time taken.

sphere

See also: hemisphere
Related word: spherical

A sphere is a perfectly round three-dimensional shape, like a ball. It has only one curved face.

square

See also: cube, parallel, parallelogram, power, quadrilateral, rectangle, rhombus
Related word: squared

Square has two meanings in maths.

a) A square is a special **rectangle** that has four sides of the same length and four angles of 90° (90 degrees). It has two pairs of opposite sides that are **parallel**.

b) To square a number means to multiply it by itself, for example 3×3. This is also shown as 3^2 and is called 'three squared' or 'three to the power of two'.

A chessboard is one big square made up of 64 smaller squares.

square centimetre

See also: area, metric

A square centimetre (cm^2) is a **metric** unit we use to measure **area**. It is $\frac{1}{10\,000}$ of a square metre.

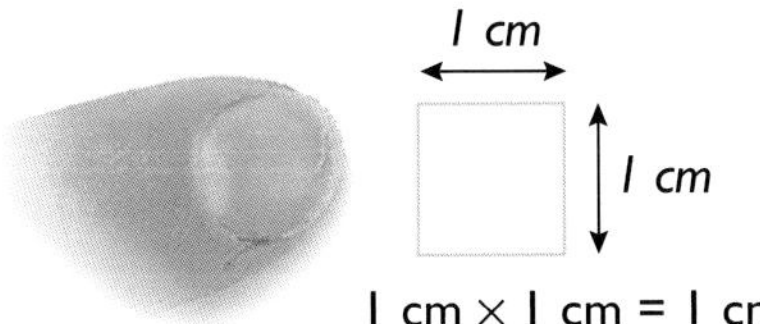

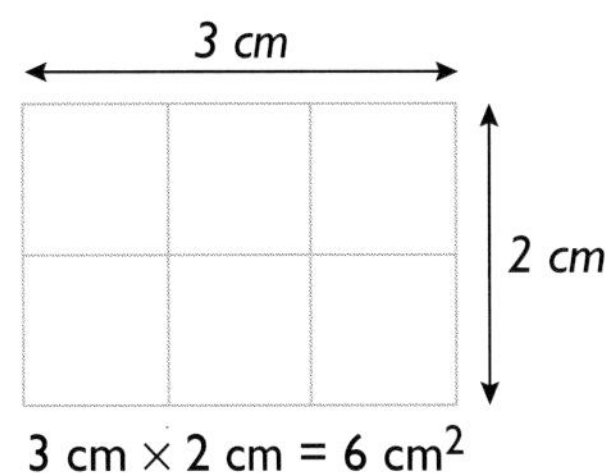

square metre

See also: area, metric

A square metre (m^2) is a **metric** unit we use to measure **area**.

$1\ m \times 1\ m = 1\ m^2$

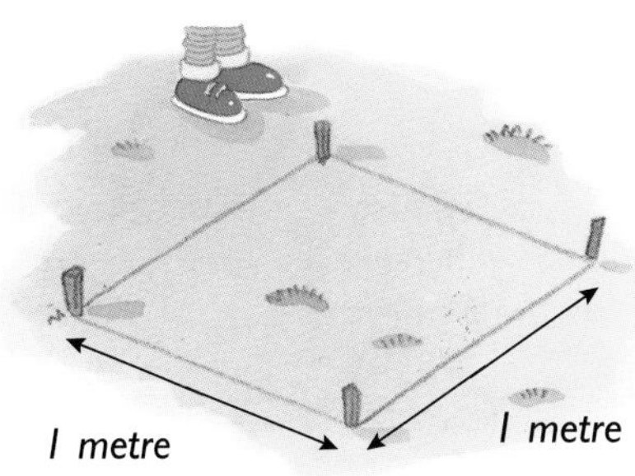

square millimetre

See also: area, metric

A square millimetre (mm^2) is a **metric** unit we use to measure **area**. It is $\frac{1}{1\,000\,000}$ of a square metre.

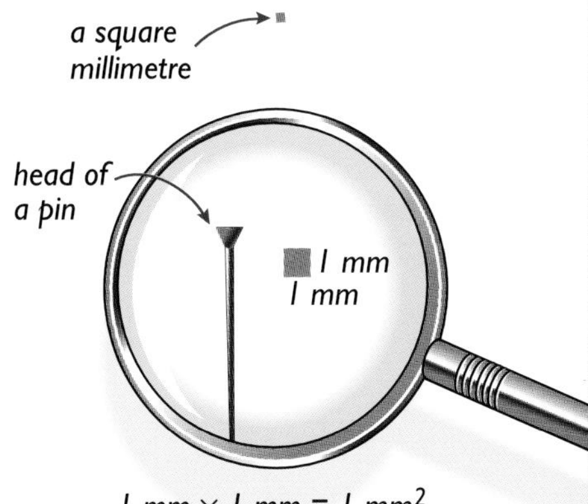

square number

See also: cubic number, triangular number

A square number is a number that can be drawn as a pattern of dots in the shape of a square. A square number is the result of multiplying a number by itself. Examples include 1, 4, 9, 16, 25 and so on.

1 (1 × 1) *4 (2 × 2)* *9 (3 × 3)* *16 (4 × 4)* *25 (5 × 5)*

square root

See also: cube root, square, square number

The square root (symbol √) of any number is the number that, when multiplied by itself, gives the first number. The square root of 64 ($\sqrt{64}$) is 8, because 8 × 8 gives 64.

stone

See also: mass, imperial

Stone (st) is an **imperial** unit for measuring **mass**. One stone is equal to fourteen pounds (lb). One stone is approximately 6·3 kilograms.

straight angle

See also: angle, turn

A straight angle is a turn of 180° (180 degrees). It is an angle whose lines have been opened out flat.

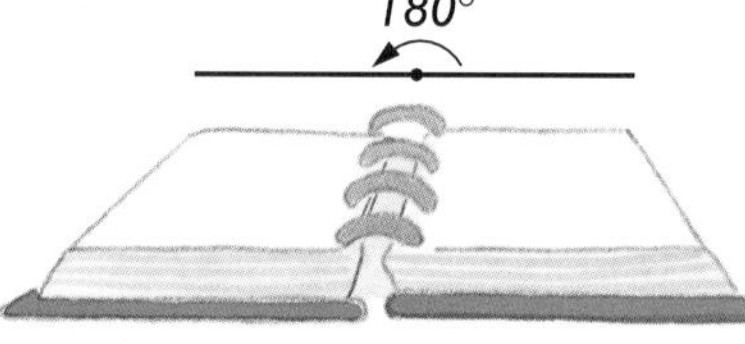

subtraction

See also: addition, difference
Related words: less, minus, subtract, take away

Subtraction means taking one number away from another or finding the **difference** between two numbers. It is the opposite of **addition**. We use the sign – to show subtraction.

sum

See also: addition, product
Related word: total

The sum is the answer we get by adding numbers together. The sum of 3 and 9 is 12.

surface area

See also: area, face

The surface area of a three-dimensional shape is the **area** of all its **faces** added together.

1 m *1.5 m* *2 m*

surface area = total of all faces

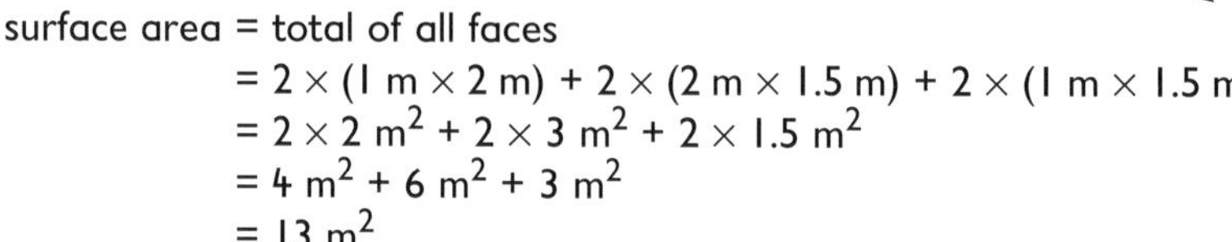

$$= 2 \times (1\text{ m} \times 2\text{ m}) + 2 \times (2\text{ m} \times 1.5\text{ m}) + 2 \times (1\text{ m} \times 1.5\text{ m})$$
$$= 2 \times 2\text{ m}^2 + 2 \times 3\text{ m}^2 + 2 \times 1.5\text{ m}^2$$
$$= 4\text{ m}^2 + 6\text{ m}^2 + 3\text{ m}^2$$
$$= 13\text{ m}^2$$

symbol

A symbol or sign is used instead of writing words. Symbols are short, easy ways of giving information. There are lots of symbols in mathematics, including +, –, ×, ÷, =, >, %, √, 2, *y*, $\frac{1}{2}$ and °.

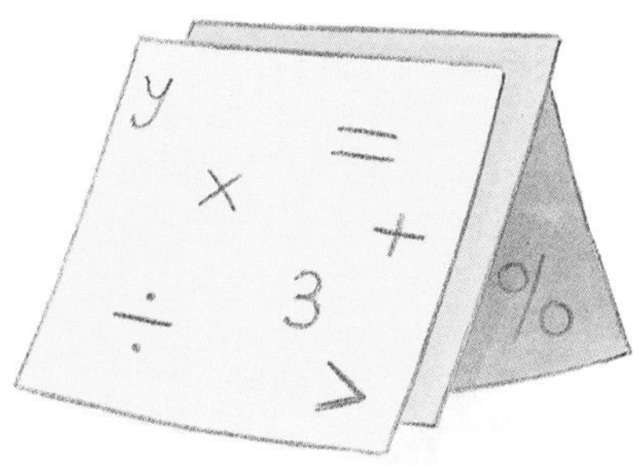

symmetry

Related word: symmetrical

There are two types of symmetry: **reflective** and **rotational symmetry**.

a) A two-dimensional shape has reflective symmetry if we can fold it along a straight line so that the two halves fit over each other exactly. A three-dimensional shape has reflective symmetry when it can be sliced into two halves that mirror each other.

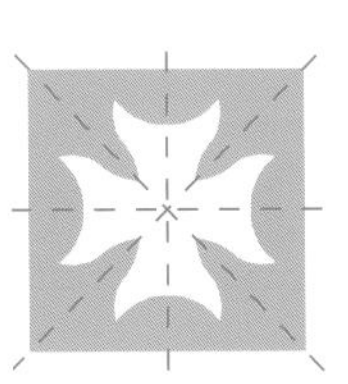

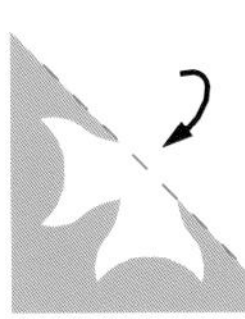
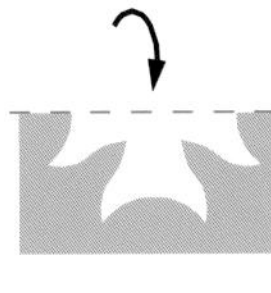
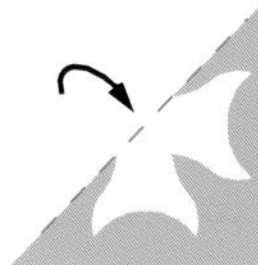

a two-dimensional shape with reflective symmetry

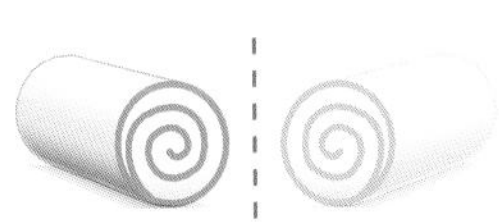

a three-dimensional object with reflective symmetry

b) A two-dimensional shape has rotational symmetry if it can fit into its outline in more than one way as it is turned through one complete turn. A three-dimensional shape has rotational symmetry when it can fit into its 'outline' in more than one way as it is rotated around a central point.

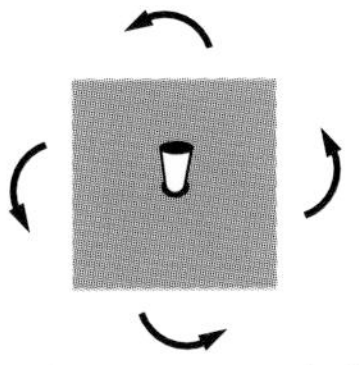

a two-dimensional shape with rotational symmetry

a three-dimensional object with rotational symmetry

take away

See also: addition
Related words: less, minus, subtract, subtraction

Take away means 'subtract' or 'minus'. Five take away three is two (5 – 3 = 2).

tally, tally chart

See also: frequency table

A tally chart is a quick way of recording information as it happens. We might use it to record the number of cars passing along a road. Tallying uses one mark (tally) for each item of information; to make it easy to count the tallies, we usually draw the fifth item across the others, like ~~||||~~.

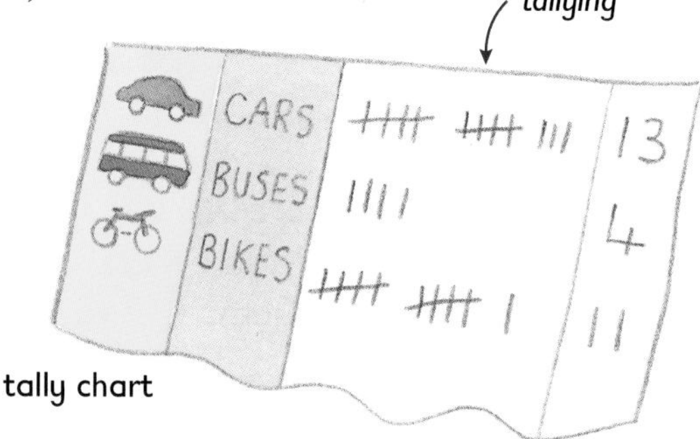

By tallying the number of items into groups of 5, we can add up the scores quickly.

tenth

A tenth is one part of something that has been divided into ten equal parts. One tenth can be written as a fraction ($\frac{1}{10}$), as a decimal (0·1) or as a percentage (10%). Tenths are written in the column to the right of the decimal point.

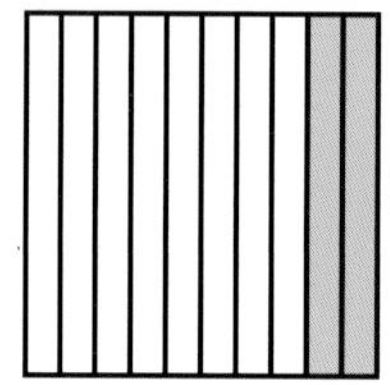

2 tenths = $\frac{2}{10}$ = 0·2

tessellation

See also: net
Related word: tessellate

Tessellation is a way of covering a surface using many of the same shapes fitted together without any gaps. Floor tiles, squared paper in your maths book and the honeycomb pattern are examples of tessellations.

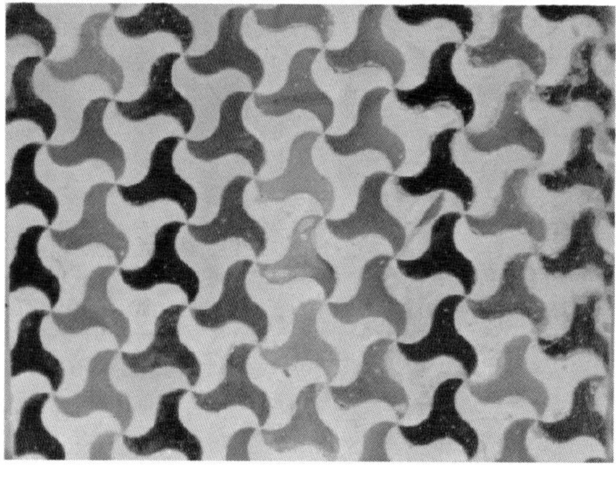

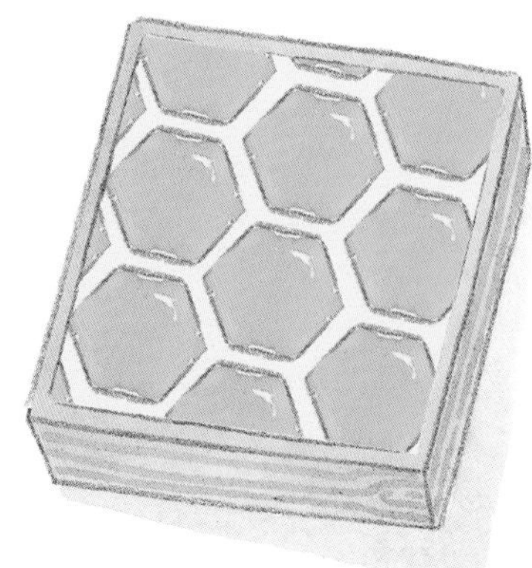

tetrahedron

See also: regular polyhedron

A tetrahedron is a three-dimensional shape that has four triangular faces. It is a pyramid with a triangular base. A regular tetrahedron has all four faces as equilateral triangles.

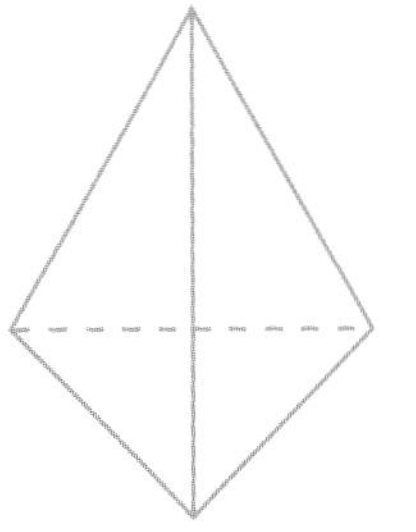

third

A third is one part of something that has been divided into three equal parts. It can be written as a fraction ($\frac{1}{3}$), a decimal ($0{\cdot}\dot{3}$) or a percentage ($33\frac{1}{3}\%$).

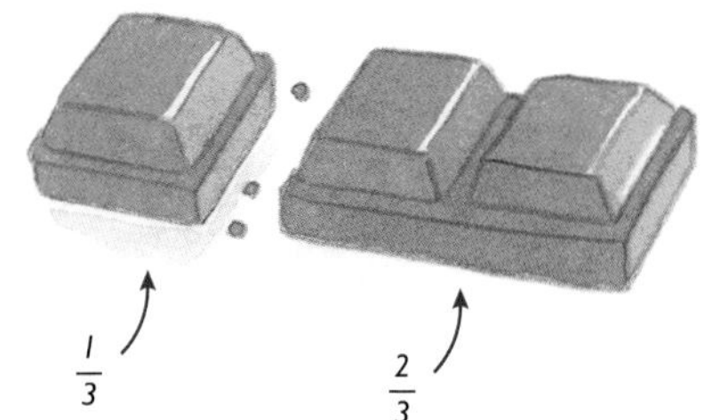

three-dimensional

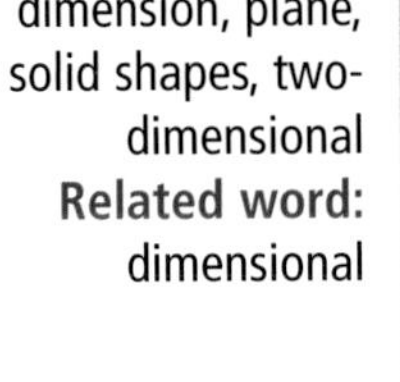
See also: dimension, plane, solid shapes, two-dimensional
Related word: dimensional

Dimensions are measurements of size and shape. Three-dimensional shapes have dimensions in three directions – they have length, width and height (or depth). They are also called 3-D shapes, and examples include cuboids, prisms and spheres. Three-dimensional shapes can be either solid or hollow.

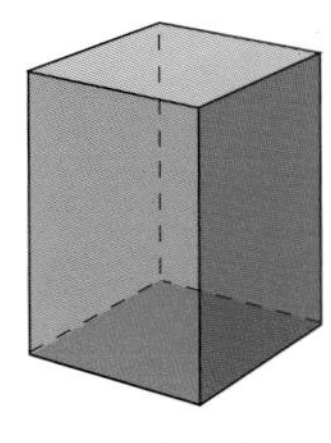
cuboid

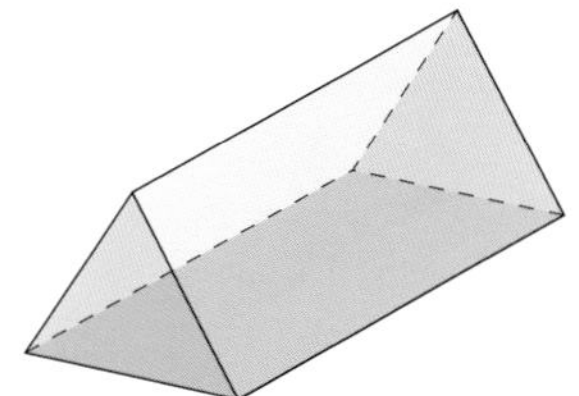
triangular prism

sphere

time

Time is a period in which things happen. We measure the passing of time in units like seconds, minutes, hours, days, weeks, months and years.

A B C D E F G H I J K L M N O P Q R S T U V W X Y Z

top-heavy fraction

See: improper fraction

total

See also: addition, sum

The total is the answer we get by adding numbers together.

transformation

See also: enlargement, reflection, rotation, translation
Related word: transform

A transformation is a way of moving or changing a shape. There are four types of transformation: **translation**, **reflection**, **rotation** and **enlargement**.

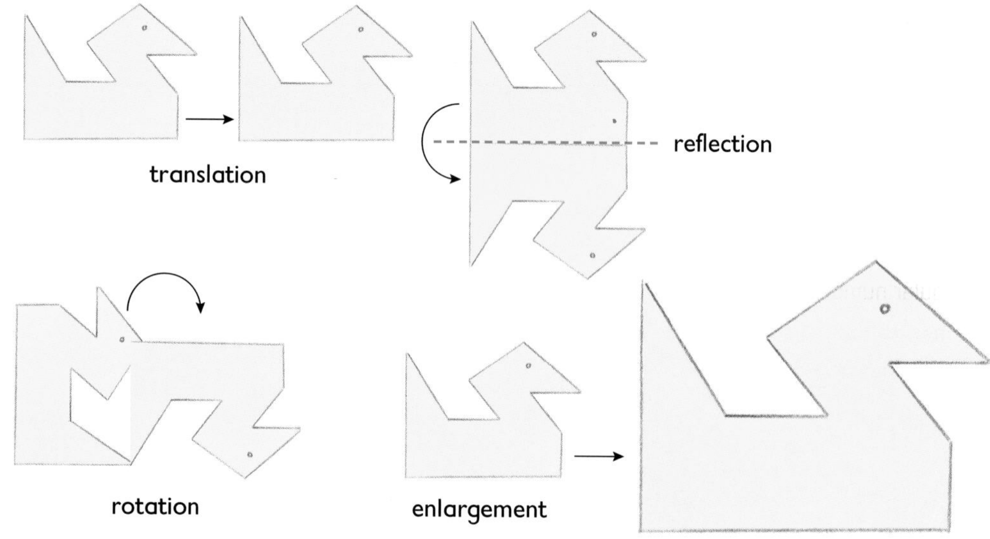

translation

See also: transformation
Related word: translate

A translation moves a shape by sliding it up, down, sideways or diagonally, without turning it or making it bigger or smaller. It is a type of **transformation.**

Each letter r, for example, in this sentence could be a translation of the first r in the sentence.

trapezium

See also: parallel, quadrilateral

A trapezium is a two-dimensional shape with four sides. One pair of sides is **parallel**, with one side longer than the other.

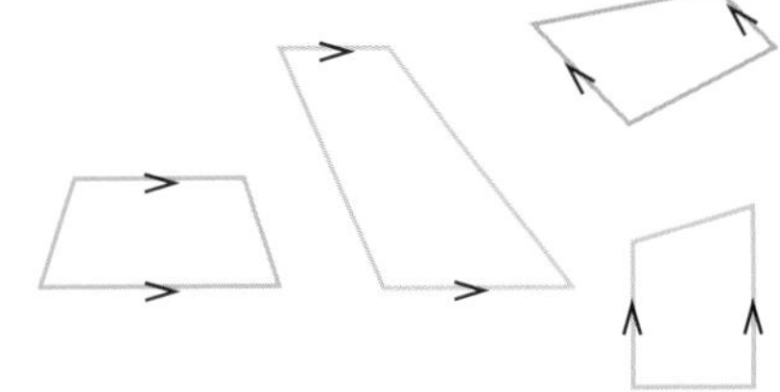

These are all trapeziums.

triangle

See also: equilateral triangle, isosceles triangle, right-angled triangle, scalene triangle
Related word: triangular

A triangle is a two-dimensional shape with three straight sides and three angles.

> There are different types of triangle called **equilateral, isosceles, scalene** and **right-angled**.

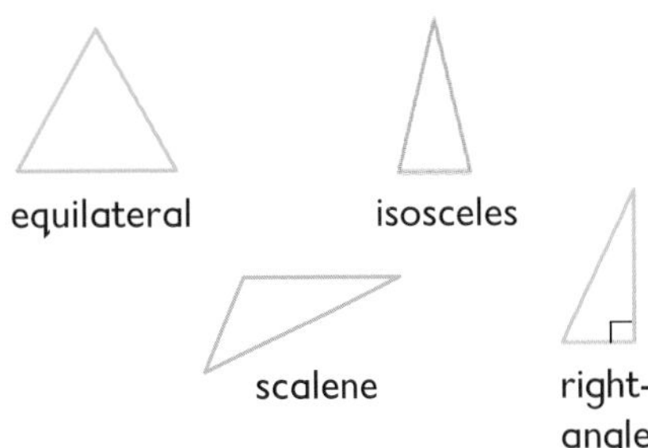

triangular number

See also: rectangular number, square number

A triangular number can be drawn as a pattern of dots which make a triangle. Examples of triangular numbers are 1, 3, 6, 10, 15 …
(1 is counted as a triangular number).

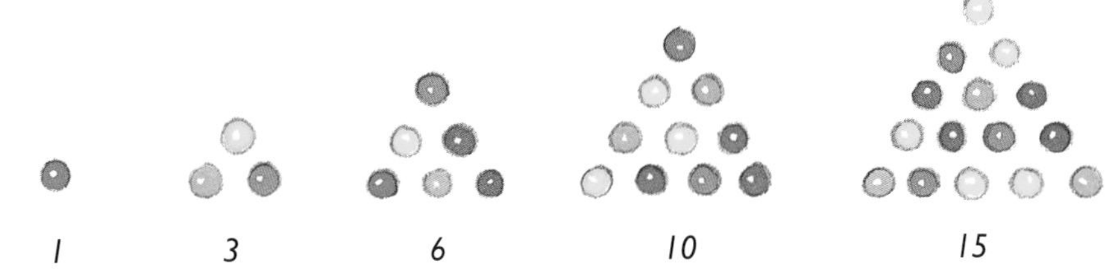

triangular prism

See also: prism, three-dimensional, triangle

A triangular prism is a three-dimensional shape that has triangular faces of the same size at each end. The cross-section parallel to the triangular faces is the same throughout the length of the prism.

turn

See also: centre of rotation, degree, half turn, quarter turn, rotation

A turn is a **rotation** which can be measured in **degrees**.

twenty-four-hour clock

See also: a.m., p.m.

A twenty-four-hour clock uses the numbers from 0 to 24 to stand for the hours in the day. The hours are counted from midnight to midnight, rather than using numbers up to twelve twice (i.e. before midday and after midday). When we write 24-hour clock times we use four digits, for example, 15:00, 21:30, 06:15, 23:05, 00:05.

Three minutes past three in the afternoon is written as 15:03 in the 24-hour clock.

Here are some 24-hour clock times written as 12-hour clock times:

- 00:05 is 12.05 a.m.
- 06:15 is 6.15 a.m.
- 15:00 is 3.00 p.m.

two-dimensional

See also: dimension, plane, three-dimensional
Related word: dimensional

Dimensions are measurements of size and shape. Two-dimensional shapes are flat, and have dimensions in two directions – length and width (or height). They are also called 2-D shapes (or plane shapes), and examples include triangles, squares, pentagons and circles.

Shapes drawn onto a piece of paper are two-dimensional as they have no depth.

unit

See also: decimal, decimal point, digit, imperial, metric, whole number

Unit has two meanings in maths.

a) In a **whole number**, the **digit** on the right is the units digit. This digit tells us how many ones, or units, we have, rather than tens, hundreds, tenths and so on. In a **decimal**, it is the digit to the left of the **decimal point**. In these numbers the units digit is in blue: 8, 1345, 37, 20, 6·2, 0·37.

Th	H	T	U	t	h
			8		
1	3	4	5		
		3	7		
		2	0		
			6	2	
			0	3	7

b) A unit of measurement tells us what we are measuring in, such as metres, grams, millilitres or seconds. When we write a measurement we must always write the unit as well, for example, 6·24 kilograms, 3·1 centimetres, 14 hours, 25 ounces. We use two systems of measurement units: **metric** and **imperial**.

unlikely

See also: equally likely outcomes, probability

In probability, unlikely means there are more chances of something not happening than happening. For example, the probability of rolling dice and getting a 6 is unlikely (there are more chances of throwing any of 1, 2, 3, 4 and 5).

Being dealt a hand of cards all the same suit is unlikely.

value

See also: place value

The value of something is what it is worth. In **place value**, the value of the two in 258 is two hundreds and the value of the two in 0·27 is two tenths. In real life, the value of a can of drink might be 40p and a car might be valued at £10 000.

variable

See also: algebra
Related word: vary

A variable is something that can change its value, that is, it is not fixed. It is often shown by a letter, as in this example $x + y = 10$. Here the value of x could be different numbers. It would be 0 if $y = 10$, or 1 if $y = 9$ and so on. Variables are often used in **algebra**.

Venn diagram

See also: Carroll diagram, intersection, set

A Venn diagram is a way of representing information using circles inside a rectangle. A circle stands for a set of things. If something belongs to two sets, the two circles will overlap or **intersect**.

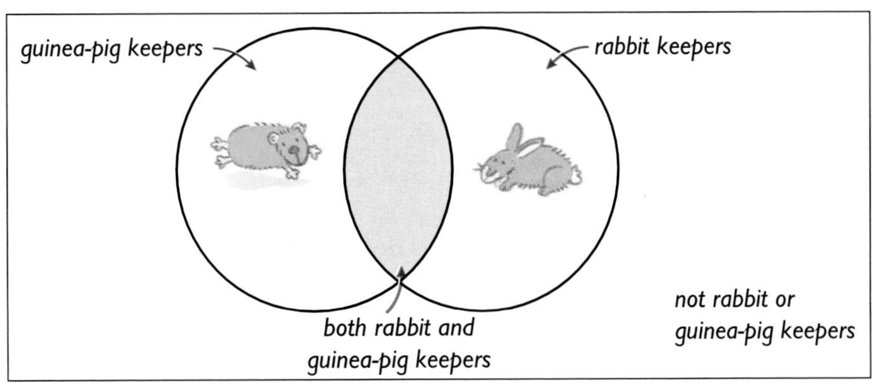

vertex

A vertex is a corner of a shape. The plural of vertex is vertices. A square has four vertices and a cube has eight.

vertical

See also: horizontal

A vertical line is a line that points straight up at 90° (90 degrees) from a **horizontal** line. We can see vertical lines in walls and doors.

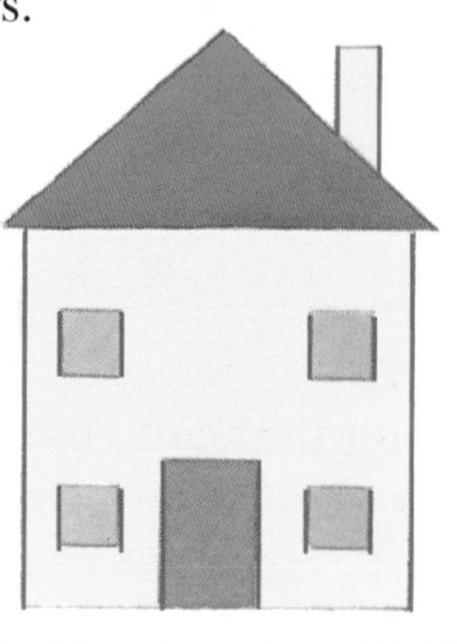

vertical line

The vertical lines have been highlighted.

volume

See also: capacity, cubic centimetre, cubic metre, litre, millilitre

Volume is a measure of how much space something takes up. We measure the volume of a three-dimensional object in **cubic centimetres** (cm^3) or **cubic metres** (m^3) or in **litres** (l), **millilitres** (ml), **pints** (pt) and **gallons** (gall).

We can measure the volume of an object in different ways. We might: build the object using cubes of known volume, or we could put it under water and measure how much the water rises or calculate it using a formula. The formula for finding the volume of a cube or cuboid is: length × width × height.

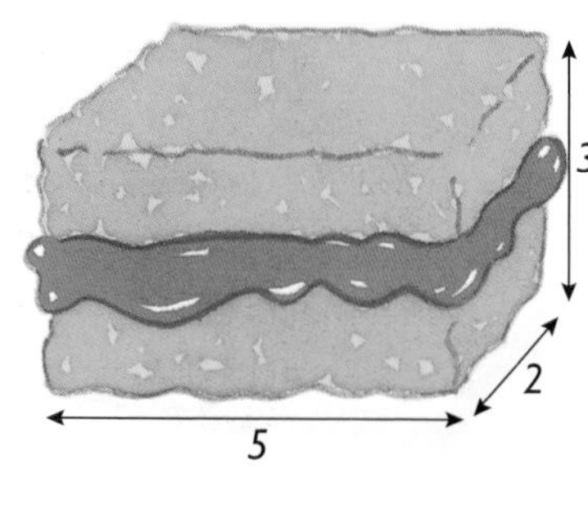

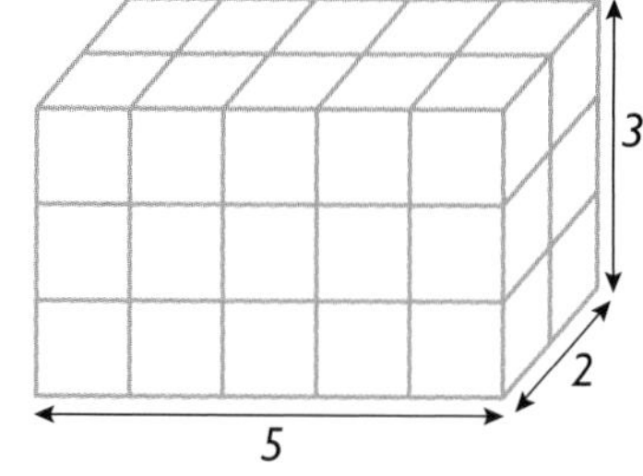

volume = 5 × 2 × 3 = 30 cubes

weight

See also: imperial units, mass, metric
Related word: weigh

The weight of something is a measure of how heavy it is. Weight is a force caused by the pull of gravity on an object, and is correctly measured in newtons. It is correct to measure **mass** in grams, kilograms, ounces, pounds and stones, but because weight and mass are connected, weight is also often measured in these units.

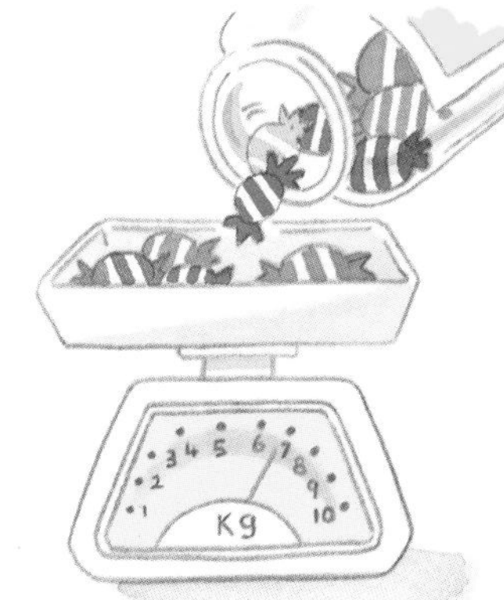

whole number

See also: integer, negative number

A whole number is any of the numbers we use for counting, including zero and negative numbers. For example, 0, 1, –4, 6, 13, –25, 364 are whole numbers but 13·6 and $-5\frac{3}{4}$ are not.

width

Related word: wide

The width of a three-dimensional object or a two-dimensional shape is the distance across it measured from side to side.

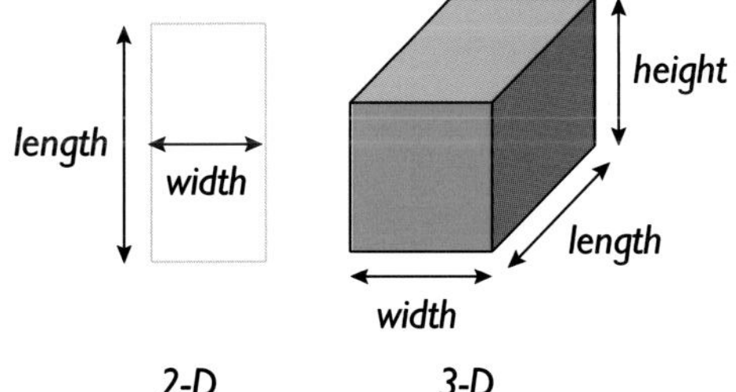

zero

Zero is sometimes called nought and is written '0'. It does several jobs in maths. In a number like 70, it shows that there are no units (otherwise the number would look like 7) and in a number like 0·04 it shows there are no units or tenths. It is also the number that separates the positive numbers from the negative numbers on a number line, as on a thermometer scale.

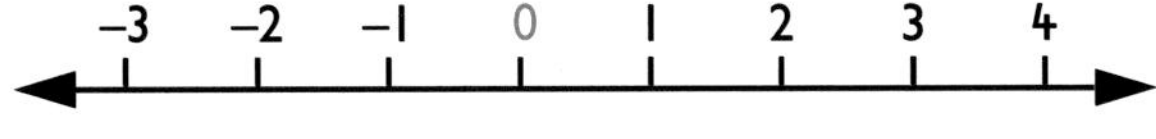

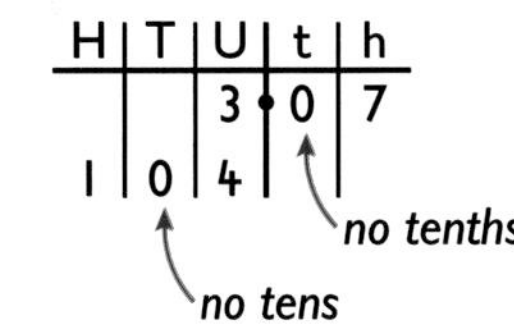